# The Mindfulness Manual

www.insightmeditation.org

Dedicated to Nadamo
(May 22 1956 - September 2 2011)
and all who engage in service to others

# An Appreciation

This is to express a deep appreciation for all those who have kindly given support to the publication of *The Mindfulness Manual*. The efforts of various people have made publication possible. People have given generously their gift of time, energy, knowledge, skills, editing, translation, preparation for publication and donations to make this book possible.

## GENEROSITY

Abide beyond in the fragrance,
Just give, a holding that empties,
in yielding such expansive ways
to meet a range of kind assemblies.
Your gift transforms a far landscape,
an act free from pursuit's return,
sublime then supports the need,
a noble form expresses its concern.
Distance becomes a union,
a gift enters uncommon space,
you lead the way to truth's domain,
a link is found, an interface.

# Contents

# A Brief Summary

## Two Modules of the Mindfulness Manual

Every chapter includes quotations from the Buddha, teachings on mindfulness, a contemporary poem by the author and practices to explore.

### Module One

**The Body. Part One**. Ethical foundations for mindfulness. Points to bear in mind for mindfulness. Mindfulness of washing-up. Mindfulness of writing. Meditation on mindfulness of breathing.

**The Body. Part Three**. Tracking your experience. Meditation on the body. Taking refuge in the Three Jewels. Benefits of mindfulness. Description of four postures. Mindfulness practice when walking. Mindfulness for stretching exercises.

**The Body. Part Four.** Working with difficulties or hindrances. Factors that contribute to inner peace. Bringing mindfulness to all possessions kept at home. Mindfulness of driving a car.

**The Feelings. Part One**. Mindfulness of grasping feelings whether pleasant, unpleasant or between pleasant and unpleasant. Natural wisdom. What feeds fear and anger?

**The Feelings. Part Two.** Meditation on feelings. 5 ways to look at meditation. 3 Avenues of meditation. Reflection on happiness.

**The Feelings. Part Three.** Areas to meditate upon. Links of dependent arising. Tendency to compare.

**The Feelings. Part Four**. Self-blame/self-doubt. Solving of problems. Meditation on painful emotions.

## Module 2

**The States of Mind. Part One.** 8 dualities of mind. Witnessing inner life. 8 ways of giving. Meditation on love/loving kindness/friendship.

**The States of Mind. Part Two.** Conditions for states of mind. The Buddha's psychological analysis. 2 kinds of thought.

**The States of Mind. Part Three.** Love of Knowledge. Knowledge and Reading. Meditation on Choiceless Awareness.

**The States of Mind. Part Four.** Problems and solutions. Liberation through non-clinging. 7 areas of mindfulness.

**The Dharma. Part One.** The exploration of teachings. Mindfulness of the past. Old karma.

**The Dharma. Part Two.** Non-self. Right Livelihood. Mindfulness at work. Contact with like-minded people

**The Dharma. Part Three**. Meditation on contentment. The Expanse of Practice. Global issues. Essential truths. Spiritual Experiences, Emptiness and Liberation.

**The Dharma. Part Four.** Relationship to time. Concerns with the future. Ageing and Death.

# The Mindfulness Manual

*Based on the Buddha's teachings on Mindfulness*

Welcome to *The Mindfulness Manual*. This Manual provides a variety of themes to reflect on and inquiry into. Readers can choose a single theme or more for the week or longer to explore and apply. You will see a series of teachings and practical exercises with regular quotes from the Buddha. There are questions for the reader at the end of each chapter. Sustained mindfulness training develops the capacity to handle a wide variety of challenging situations, and to understand more deeply the relationship of the inner life to the outer world.

In the Discourse for One in Higher Training, (Sekha Sutta. MLD 53) the Buddha said to Ananda, his personal attendant: "Speak about the ones in higher training."

Ananda said: "A noble one knows virtue, guards the doors of his sense faculties, who is moderate in eating and is devoted to wakefulness...When one is devoted to wakefulness that pertains to conduct...By realising with direct knowing, one enters upon and abides in deliverance of mind and deliverance by wisdom."
There are numerous training courses in society as a step towards a career. The Buddha regarded the training for a realised life as the higher training. This manual focuses on the "higher training", not a training for any kind of profession.

Mindfulness often acts as the first major step towards change. By bringing consciousness to bear on a particular situation, and shedding light on its characteristics, there is the opportunity for insight and understanding. Valued in all

Buddhist traditions, mindfulness is the cornerstone of the practice of the Theravada tradition. The tradition has lovingly preserved the practices of mindfulness in its monasteries for 2000 years.

We witness an ongoing growth of interest in mindfulness in the secular culture, including in education, hospitals, neuroscience, prisons, psychology and business. Psychologists and mind/body practitioners are taking training courses in the West. Mindfulness has become a vital tool for inner change for clients of psychologists including the treatment of stress, pain and depression. Management, consultancy and communication networks are learning to apply the principles of mindfulness to business.

British government reported that absence from work due to stress is greater than from sickness and back pain. The government said stress among workers in the private and public sector reduces staff morale, reduces capacity for sustained attention, places pressure on other employees while stressed employees seek alternative employment that costs a company time and money to recruit or train new staff.

Numerous books, hundreds of university theses worldwide, residential and non-residential courses, explain the practical application of mindfulness. There is a growing interest in the West in knowing the historical background of these mindfulness practices. While most Buddhist practitioners appreciate the application of mindfulness to Western institutions, there is some concern among a few Buddhist practitioners that Western society has amputated the limb of mindfulness from the full body of the Dharma.

The Mindfulness Manual bridges the gap. The teachings of the Buddha form a backbone to The Mindfulness Manual. It is a unique feature of the Manual with regular quotes of the Buddha throughout.

In one of his most cherished discourses, the Buddha referred to the four applications of mindfulness, as body, feelings, states of mind and the Dharma. The Dharma here refers to the teachings and practices but also all objects, material and mental, known and unknown. Everything is a Dharma. This training manual will take you through the four applications of mindfulness.

We offer a Mindfulness Training Course with mentors. Mentors and students, who join the MTC, can adapt between them the structure, form and exploration of the course. May this manual provide beneficial in your daily life to all readers.

# Features of the Mindfulness Manual

Many of the mindfulness practices will fit in with the usual rhythms of your daily life. You will benefit further if you create time for formal meditation. Basic meditation instructions are included in the mindful.

Step-by-step, this manual will guide you through the essential features of mindfulness practice. Wholesome intention serves as an important supportive factor for mindfulness. Mindfulness contributes to insight, clarity of mind, opening of the heart, awakening and liberation. It is important that you do not try to run ahead of yourself, so to speak, and instead attend to one page at a time, one section at a time, after reading the book.

The company of likeminded people provide a pillar for inner development. It is worthwhile to check out if there are any groups engaged in mindfulness practice in your area.

The Manual offers the necessary tools to find wisdom in the face of events. Just as the carpenter, plumber and electrician use tools for their trade and develop skills to apply these tools, so we use tools and develop skills to live with clear comprehension and understanding.

It would be worthwhile to keep a journal of your mindfulness experiences from one week to the next. You might keep the journal beside our bed or on the breakfast table or a small diary in our pocket. To keep a journal, you must be completely honest with yourselves.

The purpose of the journal includes to:

- *acknowledge the most difficult moments*
- *appreciate the beautiful moments of the day*
- *develop what needs to be developed*
- *explore a wise attitude to circumstances*
- *overcome what needs to be overcome*
- *question fear and anger*
- *reflect on what matters*
- *see the wise alternatives*

**In the first set of four chapters on Mindfulness of the Body,** the Manual offers basic guidelines on fundamental ethics, mindfulness of breath, diet, four postures, and our relationship to the whole of the body. We provide simple and clear instructions, quotations from the Buddha, a summary of practices for the week, a poem and a simple chart to report your practice.

**In the second set of four chapters on Mindfulness of Feelings,** the Manual offers teachings and practices on mindfulness of feelings. Feelings include the whole range of pleasant feelings, painful feelings and the feelings in between the two. There are both worldly feelings and spiritual feelings. There are guided meditations on feelings. We include the practice of working with difficult emotions. We look at the way feelings influence thoughts and the way feelings feed stories.

**In the third set of four chapters on Mindfulness of States of Mind**, the Manual applies mindfulness to states of mind. At times, we experience wanting, neediness and dependency on results. At other times, we experience calmness of mind, genuine contentment and we abide free from demands upon others and ourselves. Our state of mind influences what we say, what we do and what we believe.

**In the fourth set of four chapters, Mindfulness of the Dharma**, the Manual includes basic knowledge of the Buddha's teachings, including the triple gem, four truths of the noble ones, the noble path, five aggregates and the inner and outer life. This last section will include mindfulness of environmental issues and ways we can contribute to the welfare of others.

At the end of the Manual, we invite you to reflect on what developed for you and what needs further development. You may experience areas where little or no effort is required to apply mindfulness. You may also see the areas where skilful effort and the creative energy are necessary to bring more mindfulness and concentration to specific areas of your life. Make use of mindful reading of books, articles and website information.

You may wish to join our online Mindfulness Training Course (MTC) with a weekly online exchange with a personal mentor. You will find all the necessary information about the Course on www.mindfulnesstrainingcourse.org .

For further information contact:
coordinator@mindfulnesstrainingcourse.org

We appreciate your interest to explore the power of mindfulness and the wider benefits available through skilful application.

It is our intention that all practitioners come to realise the wealth of possibility that can open up when we live a truly mindful and enquiring life. In this Manual, we apply the principles of mindfulness to inner and outer issues.

*May all beings live mindful lives*
*May all beings live with insight*
*May all beings live with a liberating wisdom*

# The Buddha's Words on Mindfulness

**DN 2.21.** In walking, standing, sitting, lying down, in waking, in speaking and in keeping silent, one acts with clear awareness. In this way, one is accomplished in mindfulness and clear comprehension.

**DN 22.2.** One sits down cross-legged, holding body erect, having established mindfulness before him/her. Mindfully s/he breathes in, mindfully s/he breathes out.

**M. 53.16.** S/he has the highest mindfulness and skill; s/he recalls and recollects what was done long ago and spoken long ago.

**M 66.16.** When he is practising the way, memories and intentions associated with accumulations beset him now and then through lapses of mindfulness. His or her mindfulness may be slow to arising but s/he quickly abandoned them, removes them and does away with them

**M 118.13.** One abides contemplating the body as a body, ardent, fully aware, and mindful, having put away covetousness and grief.

**M 118.30.** The mindfulness enlightenment factor is aroused and one develops it, and by development, it comes to fulfilment.

**M. 118.33.** These three states circle around right livelihood, that is, right view, right effort, and right mindfulness.

**M. 10.46.** If anyone should develop these four foundations of mindfulness final knowing (of liberation), here and now or if there is any trace of clinging left, there is no returning though to a mundane state.

**M. 44.12.** Unification of mind is concentration. The four foundations of mindfulness (body, feelings, states of mind and Dharma) are the basis for concentration.

**M. 103.3.** In the four foundations of mindfulness you should all train in concord, with mutual appreciation, without disputing.

**M. 118.12.** In this Sangha (community of practitioners), there are those who abide devoted to the development of the four foundations of mindfulness.

**M. 151.12.** If by reviewing, he knows that the four foundations of mindfulness are not developed in me, then he should make an effort to develop them. If by reviewing, he knows the four foundations of mindfulness are developed in me, then he can abide happy and glad training day and night in wholesome states.

**M. 62.5.** Develop mindfulness of breathing. When mindfulness of breathing is developed and cultivated, it is of great fruit and great benefit.

**M. 141.30.** What is right mindfulness? One contemplates the body as a body, feelings as feelings, states of mind as states of mind, and Dharma as Dharma having put away covetousness and grief for the world.

**SN. 1.130.** A person has various foodstuffs strewn over his lap – sesame seeds, rice grains, lakes and jujubes - if he loses his mindfulness when rising from that seat he would scatter them all over.

**AN. 499.** One bent on his own welfare should practice mindfulness and guarding of the mind.

**AN. 737.** Guard the doors of the senses. Take mindfulness as protector. Be mindful and alert. A mind is under the protection of mindfulness.

**AN. 822.** One who falls asleep mindfully and with clear comprehension does not have bad dreams.

**AN. 1009.** One has a strong commitment to mindfulness and alertness and does not lose this fondness for mindfulness and alertness in the future

**AN. 1078.** With mindfulness as his gatekeeper, the noble one abandoned the unwholesome and develops the wholesome, abandoned what is blameworthy and develops what is blameless.

**AN 1160.** The Dharma is the one with mindfulness established, not for one who is muddled headed,.

**AN.611.** How is mindfulness an authority? Once mindfulness is established internally: "In just such a way, I will experience through liberation the Dharma that I have not yet experienced or assist with wisdom in various respects the Dharma that I have experienced." It is in this way that mindfulness is an authority.

**AN. 1269.** What exercises authority over intentions and thoughts? Mindfulness exercises authority over them. " "What is their supervisor?" "Wisdom is their supervisor." "What is their core?" "Liberation is their core."

**Sn. 45.** If one finds a wise friend, a companion, who is living according to wholesome virtues, then live with him happily and mindfully.

**Sn. 151**. As long as s/he is awake, s/he should develop this mindfulness.

**Sn 212**. One who has the strength of wisdom, born of ethics and restraint, tranquil in mind and delights in meditation, who is mindful, free from clinging, is called a sage by the wise.

**Sn.283**. Be pure and associate with the pure; being mindful, united and arise; put an end to suffering.

**Sn. 340**. Be restrained in the senses. Be mindful of the body. Continually develop to end fuelling what arises.

**Sn. 413**. The beggar walked on from house to house watching the sense doors, well restrained, alert and mindful. Soon his bowl was full.

**Sn 777**. Look at those who struggle after their petty ambitions, like fish in the stream that is fast drying up. Mindful, let one fair unselfish while ceasing to worry about various states of becoming.

**Sn.974**. Let him mindfully trained to end the pollution from forms, sounds, tastes, smells and touch

**Sn. 975**. Let one who is mindful with well liberated mind subdue the desire for things. Then, investigating the truth thoroughly, and with concentration, one will destroy the darkness (of not seeing).

1.     **MN. Middle Length Discourses of the Buddha.** 1150 pages plus notes etc.

2.     **DN. The Long Discourses of the Buddha.** 520 pages, plus notes etc.

3.     **AN. The Book of the Gradual Discourses** 1400 pages, plus notes etc.

4.     **SN. Connected Discourses of the Buddha** 2920 pages plus notes etc.

5.     **Sn. Sutta-Nipata. 1149 verses.**

# The Power of Mindfulness

The Power of Mindfulness (in alphabetical order):

1.    Mindful sees clearly the present and our direction.
2.    Mindfulness applies equally to being and doing.
3.    Mindfulness contributes to inner steadiness when faced with difficulties.
4.    Mindfulness embraces the general and the specific, the bigger picture and the detail.
5.    Mindfulness examines intention, action and result. Mindfulness responds to what is.
6.    Mindfulness includes the art of total listening to discern what is valuable and insightful.
7.    Mindfulness is a limb in the body of total awakening.
8.    Mindfulness is a mental faculty and a power of mind to develop.
9.    Mindfulness is a tool to transform self-centred pursuit of pleasure, negativity and fear.
10.    Mindfulness makes wise judgements and prevents the manipulation of our attention.
11.    Mindfulness of others' contribution develops and expresses appreciation and gratitude.
12.    Mindfulness refers to four applications, body, feelings, states of mind and Dharma.
13.    Mindfulness refers to our capacity to see clearly what is happening.
14.    Mindfulness reveals a clear comprehension of change, initiated or not.
15.    Mindfulness reveals what is common between self and others.
16.    Mindfulness saves falling prey to selfish desire, exploitation and indifference.

17. Mindfulness serves as an important step towards overcoming grief, despair and pain.
18. Mindfulness shows a genuine sense of responsibility for what we know.
19. Mindfulness with inquiry examines causes and conditions for suffering.
20. Mindfulness works to reduce stress, anxiety and physical pain.
21. Mindfulness, awareness or clear attention can mean inter-changeable concepts.
22. Right mindfulness includes wholesome intentions to inquire into suffering.
23. The Buddha distinguished right or healthy mindfulness from harmful mindfulness.
24. The Buddha said: "Mindfulness is applied to the extent necessary in order to abide without needing to lean on anything in the world" - either inwardly or outwardly.
25. Wholesome intentions give support to mindfulness to inquire and change situations, inner and outer, personal and institutional.

*May all beings live a mindful life*
*May all beings live with insight*
*May all beings live an awakened life*

# Mindfulness of Body - Part One

We begin with the challenge of bringing mindfulness to our relationship to ethics. That does not mean that we engage in beliefs as either moral absolutes or moral relativity. Mindfulness training includes the practice of reflection and inquiry into our views and actions.

Ethics is one of the indispensable limbs of mindfulness practice. A burglar or compulsive gambler may show strong mindfulness in his or her desire to make gains but may cause much anguish to others and themselves. Other limbs of the Dharma include concentration, equanimity, happiness, love and wisdom.

We consider our body, speech and mind in relationship to the practice of ethics. We develop ethics so we treat others as we wish to be treated, and treat ourselves with respect. These are the basic ethics that the Buddha expounded. We bring mindfulness to bear on the various ethical issues that we face.

## Five Ethical Foundations

*I undertake the practice not to engage in killing or violence.*
*I undertake the practice not to engage in stealing or cheating.*
*I undertake the practice not to engage in sexual abuse.*
*I undertake the practice not to engage in lying and harmful speech.*
*I undertake the practice not to engage in alcohol or drug abuse.*

Consider the importance of the first ethical guideline. Last year, BBC news reported that more than 300,000 US soldiers out of 2,000,000 million deployed to Iraq and Afghanistan between 2001 and 2010 have subsequently suffered from post traumatic stress disorder (PTSD) or depression. Soldiers have witnessed terrible suffering, inflicted terrible suffering on the people of Iraq and Afghanistan and often live in fear while on active duty for their fellow soldiers and themselves. Some soldiers and their officers live with terrible guilt and nightmares over their actions. Soldiers have returned home from active duty and engaged in domestic violence, become alcoholics and some have committed suicide. The Buddha made it clear that ethics, mindfulness and wise action serve as the very foundation to reduce stress. Ethics are indispensable to mindfulness practices.

It is worthwhile to remember these five ethics. We can inquire deeply into ourselves whether we:

- *condone war, executions and destruction of human life*
- *go for what we want, regardless of personal, social or environmental cost*
- *manipulate another for sex*
- *speak without regard for facts or feelings*
- *distort the balance of our mind through intoxicants*

A wise relationship to ethics dissolves much suffering and stress. Those who engage in

- *killing – a risk of much more exposure to violence and death*
- *stealing - never knowing peace of mind*
- *sexual abuse - corrupts the inner, violates another (s) with lasting impact*
- *lying – never trusted and experiences loss of friendship*
- *abuse of alcohol and drugs - loss of clarity, despair and ill health.*

**Mindfulness of Breathing**

Mindfulness of Breathing serves as an anchor point in mindfulness training. A few mindful breaths can give us the necessary breathing space before we express certain views or embark on an action. We bring mindfulness to bear on our breaths to reduce stress, to relax and practise focussing.

Points to bear in Mind for the Application of Mindfulness

- *Mindfulness often includes the deliberate intention to focus on a particular object.*

- *As we develop the capacity to sustain our attention on an object, it means we also cultivate concentration through successive moment-to-moment application of mindfulness.*

- *Mindfulness makes direct contact with the object with a minimum number of views, labels and judgements.*

- *We take notice of characteristics of the object of interest. One important characteristic is impermanence, the capacity to be mindful of changes, gross and subtle, in what we perceive.*

Mindfulness brings a power to the mind. We reduce the influence of our habits that disconnects us from the immediacy of the present moment.

We often fail to realise the way stress and pressure build up through showing little real interest in the immediacy of unfolding events. For example, we felt bored and then suddenly over reacted to a situation. We had not noticed resistance building up within.

The quality of moment-to-moment attention and the power of concentration contribute significantly to the interruption of these unhealthy patterns so that we feel a genuine connection with the task, no matter how small.

We have probably all hurried through washing up the dishes to get them finished so we can get on with something else. The same attitude may apply to other areas of our life. Mindfulness of dishwashing contributes to calm, relaxation and insight into various tasks.

This Mindfulness Training programme includes a range of practical tasks at home, outdoors and indoors, including the shopping mall, office and walking along the pavement. It is important to apply mindfulness to the minor events of our daily life. We spend many hours daily in taking care of the body. Getting dressed and undressed, brushing teeth, washing, a shower, shaving, eating, going to the toilet and possibly using cosmetics.

Mindfulness requires a certain discipline to stay focused on what we do. For example, if you give full attention to the washing up, it means you let go of resistance, hurrying to get things done and the desire to be somewhere else. The same principle applies if you use a washing machine. Be mindful of energy expenditure if using an electrical appliance.

**Mindfulness of Washing-up**

- *Make a clear intention to be mindful from picking up the cutlery to place in the sink.*

- *Be mindful of the contact of your hands with the items.*
- *Be mindful of your hand turning the tap on and the water going into the sink.*

- *Make it a slow easy process so that each step of the way deserves real attention.*

- *After washing the dishes, dry them and put the various items back in the drawers and cupboards.*

- *Be mindful of the various sensations in your body as you bend and stretch.*

- *When everything is clean and tidy, then stand still for a few moments and be mindful of the completed task.*

- *Be mindful that the task had a beginning, middle and end to it.*

- *Allow your whole being to stand there in the kitchen a few moments to acknowledge completion before you move on to something else.*

Remember to engage in this practice on a daily basis. If you notice you are speeding up, then purposefully slow down to reconnect with the task.

**Mindfulness of Writing**

Reflection is an important tool of mindfulness training. It requires the capacity to look back over the immediate past to acknowledge the benefits of a particular practice. Check out what needs further development and what constitutes the greatest difficulty.

We wish to encourage you to keep a brief report of your experiences so that you can share them with your mentor. We have provided a chart for each week for your reflections. Feel free to add blank pages and write more and share with your mentor whatever you wish.

It is important that you endeavour to be as accurate and precise as possible. We sometimes can have the tendency when we write to exaggerate the positive or the negative and both those inhibit the opportunity to reflect rather precisely our first hand experience. It is worthwhile to practise writing slowly, neatly and mindfully rather than a hurried scribble.

**Practice of Mindfulness of Breathing**

- *In the sitting posture, be mindful of the full breath experience.*
- *Experience the body expanding with the inhalation and contracting with the exhalation.*
- *Be mindful of breathing in and breathing out.*
- *If tired, keep the eyes open. If restless, breathe long and deep, relax with the out breath.*
- *Allow the breath to flow in and out of the body, shallow or deep.*
- *Be aware of any moment(s) of stillness before the next in-breath.*
- *Be aware of changes in the breath, of impermanence of every breath.*
- *Experience the air element stimulating the cells of the body.*

- *Relax gently with the out breath when the mind easily wanders.*
- *Let the brain cells become quiet.*
- *Air element confirms our intimacy and inter-dependence with the surrounding world.*
- *Feel the freedom of simply breathing in and breathing out.*
- *Mindfulness of breathing contributes to harmony of body and mind*
- *Mindfulness connects directly with organic life.*

## Words of the Buddha

*"What is right (fulfilling) mindfulness? One abides contemplating body as body, ardent, clearly aware and mindful, have put aside hankering and fretting…*

*One abides contemplating feelings as feelings.*

*One abides contemplating states of mind as states of mind.*

*One abides contemplating Dharma as Dharma, ardent, clearly aware and mindful, having put aside longing and fretting…"*

*"Remaining imperturbable, mindful and clearly aware, he experiences himself joy". (DN22)*

## I WAKE UP

I wake this special morning. Life is now
e'er fresh, with sunny home, with none about,

I am awake, this realm alone to bow.
I'm life! I'm here! I know the joy to shout,
and wonder what the risks and what the play,
angel abroad, a small town dweller's manual.
I wake up! Light falls here. Delight to say.
This sky! This world! This marvel tour de force!

Allow eyelids to flicker, sights arrive,
A new day! Dress, brush teeth, plus tea and toast,
divine daylight, and  birdsong comes alive,
a  new day travels, sense of real comes close,
a call engaged; fresh explorations near.
I have been born anew, this timeless beat,
I can't explain what my perceptions fear,
a doorbell rings and I take steps to greet.

---

**The Practices**

**1. Practise mindfulness of dish washing daily**

**2. Practise daily mindful breathing for 10 to 15 minutes**

**3. Start the day in a mindful way from waking up**

**4. Employ long, deep in and out breaths to abide calmly**

**5. Read, reflect and write on ethical practices.**

**Write in box times of formal practice.**

**Write type of practice and brief reflection on it.**

| Monday | |
|---|---|
| Tuesday | |
| Wednesday | |
| Thursday | |
| Friday | |
| Saturday | |
| Sunday | |

# Mindfulness of the Body - Part Two

### The Problem with Stress

Stress and being busy, let alone very busy, often have a direct relationship. We can also experience stress when we have nothing to do and do not know what to do.

The experience of pressure around a partner, children, money, work, study, tasks and unresolved issues generate stress. We can summarise stress in numerous ways.

- *Desire to get things done*
- *Fear of not getting things done*
- *Waiting for an outcome in the future*
- *Feeling misunderstood or rejected*
- *Placing unfulfilled expectations upon ourselves.*
- *Projecting into a situation*
- *Thinking too much about something.*

Some of you who have embarked on this three month manual may already interpret this training manual as yet one more thing to do. "I am already so busy. I haven't got time to engage in a mindfulness programme, even though it is designed to serve my deeper interests." To put it in another way, "I haven't got time to reduce my stress even though I am experiencing so much stress."

We then return to our stressful way of life forgetting that stress has a painful impact on feelings, emotions, thoughts and our engagement with others in personal, social and working life. Stress can lead to exhaustion, burn out, despair and sickness in our efforts to get everything done that we want to do.

A common stressful thought is, "I don't have time." If we hear ourselves say this in our thoughts or to others, let us take this as a signal of stress. Take three to five minutes to breathe in and out. Quietly inquire into our priorities. A full life is different from a busy life. A full and creative life emerges for those free from stress. Stress is the hindrance to a full life.

Some claim: "I need stress to get things done. I need to put pressure on myself and I need pressure from others to get things done." In the Dharma teachings, we need wise intention, interest and love to achieve goals, not living in constant pressure.

We believe this manual will make this exceptionally clear to you through your own experience.

### The Pali Word for Mindfulness

The Pali word for mindfulness is *sati*. *Sati* comes from a root word that means "to remember" and implies a genuine presence of mind, an act of remembering to see what reveals itself. Sati embraces the present and remembers conditions, due to past. To be mindful means to be conscious of what is past, present or future, abstract thinking or deep experiences. With mindfulness, we are able to recall the past, examine the present and pay wise attention to the future.

Past experiences give us the opportunity to learn from the past. Mindfulness does not reject the past but enables the clarity from the past to inform the present.

It is valuable to bear in mind the qualities that give support to mindfulness, namely the power to retain insights, clear views and a lucid attention.

**Five-Minute Meditation on Experience of the Hands**

We use our hands to express our state of mind. We can employ our hands to express love in various ways, creativity and calmness. We can also use the hands to express greed, anger and confusion. Mindful practice of this part of the body can transform the inner life.

- *Place your hands in your lap, with the two thumbs touching each other.*
- *Make sure your back is straight and that you are sitting comfortably.*
- *Relax into this position. Gently hold this position for five minutes,*
- *Keep the body as calm as possible.*
- *Direct your mindfulness to the sensations in your hands.*
- *Notice whether they are tense or relaxed, warm or cool, dry or moist.*
- *Practise this technique daily in any suitable environment.*
- *Be mindful of any movement in your hands due to a state of mind.*

**Mindfulness of Breathing When Seated**

The next time you remain seated for several minutes or more, rather than reading a newspaper or watching television, give the time to mindfulness of breathing. The path to full awareness begins with a single breath.

- *Keep the posture upright. Sit tall.*

- *Make the breath a little longer and deeper than usual for the first couple of minutes*
- *Experience the expansion of the body as the oxygen enters*
- *And the settling down as the body expels the carbon dioxide,*
- *Try to experience as many breaths as possible during this period*
- *Remember that the mind most easily wanders on the out-breath*
- *Experience moments of stillness before the body draws in the next in-breath*
- *Experience the one whole breath from start to finish and then the next*
- *Trust that the body will draw in and release the amount of air it needs*
- *Experiencing conscious life breathing in and breathing out.*

## Breathing Mindfully under Pressure

Physical activity and inactivity affects the breath. State of mind affects the breath – calm, excitement, fear, happiness and anger. We practise to experience the breath directly noticing when we are relaxed or when we experience stress.

Mindfulness of breathing helps us to work with and work through pain and agitation. We need to remember that practice develops the mind, not theory.

Practise mindfulness of breathing to be calm and relaxed in the here and now but also as a support for our goals. The practice contributes to initiating a task rather than daydreaming or avoiding. We mindfully breathe in an out to focus and then act rather than procrastinate.

- *When troubled, then breathe in and breathe out deeply.*
- *Place plenty of attention on the outgoing breath and relax into the out breath.*

- *If you feel yourself holding back unnecessarily from a situation, breathe through fear and then act.*
- *If you hear unkind words to your face, mindfully breathe in and out rather than reactive.*
- *Do not give authority to others over your state of mind.*

## Sources for Insight

A genuine insight frees the mind up, opens the heart and transforms perceptions. Insights can run deep, affecting the very cells of our being. Reading about the experience of others is no substitute, yet one sentence in a book can change our lives.

Insights contribute to living with wisdom in facing what arises. Here is a list of sources for insights. Are there any areas below that you need to develop?

1. *Discussion*
2. *Focussed attention*
3. *Inquiry*
4. *Listening*
5. *Meditation*
6. *Mindful living*
7. *Nature*
8. *Reading*
9. *Receptivity*
10. *Reflection*
11. *Speaking*
12. *Spontaneous arising*

Invaluable insights can come from experience, beautiful and ugly, pleasurable and painful and through the most mundane of events. Benefits from insights may come immediately or much, much later. Mindfulness is the bridge to insights.

## Mindfulness of Eating

Generally speaking, the Buddhist tradition has not emphasised the importance of applied mindfulness to diet in daily life though Buddhist retreats offer a highly nutritious vegetarian diet. A nutritious diet feeds body *and* mind. Certain foods have an impact on our health and attitudes. It is worth being mindful of our consumption of sugar, salt and fat often found in packaged foods. See Environmental Ethics on Menu of home page of www.mindfulnesstrainingcourse.org

- *Are the plants and fruit trees organically grown, sprayed with chemicals or genetically modified?*
- *Be conscious of each mouthful of food. Endeavour to experience the food almost as liquid before swallowing.*
- *Be mindful of what you eat.*
- *Before eating, reflect on the food chain.*
- *Do we eat anything with a face - animals, birds or fish?*
- *Does the ethic of being a vegetarian or vegan contribute to our health and welfare of creatures?*
- *Does the ethic of being vegetarian or vegan contribute to wise use of farming land?*
- *Give thanks for the opportunity to eat in a hungy world for more than a billion people*
- *How much do we eat?*
- *Is our diet nutritious? Is it imported? Is it nationally or locally grown?*
- *Remember to leave some space in the stomach so that the food can convert easily into energy.*
- *Try to ensure that you do not waste food.*
- *What do we say no to due to food, method of farming or the food corporation*

*Due to globalisation, an item of food travels on average more than 1000 kilometres before it reaches the kitchen table. Remember the farmers, farm workers, distributors, supermarkets, shops and market stalls that have made it possible to take the meal.*

## The Practice of Mindful Eating

The Buddha found little necessity to pay attention to diet in a time of healthy, organic food.

There are four considerations with regard to food. All four matter equally. They are:

- *What we eat and drink*
- *The amount that we eat and drink*
- *The quality of mindfulness when we eat and drink*
- *The emotional influences at the time we eat and drink*

If we can bear in mind each of these four areas, we can discover a balanced relationship to food, rather than through overeating, under-eating, compulsive eating or anxiety around food.

## Exercise

A family doctor told me that some of his patients confessed their heart only beat faster when they were anxious or afraid. In Britain, a unit of exercise consists of 20 minutes where the heart beats faster than usual owing to the movement of the body. It can take many forms – from fast walking, gardening, to a parent carrying their child around. Experience two units or more a day to increase deliberately your heart beat.

- *Are you willing to include exercise into daily life?*
- *How many units of exercise do you engage in over a week?*

- *Do you make time, for example, for 40 minutes per day of fast walking?*
- *Do you stretch out the body in different ways or just sit and walk?*
- *Do you keep fit through contact with others committed to fitness and well-being?*

## The Posture

The Buddha encouraged us to "sit with a straight back, and meditate." If we were to see a skeleton of our self, we would probably be alarmed at some of the typical postures that we adopt. Poor posture distorts the spine, creates pressure in various parts of the body and leads to pressure upon the organs including heart, liver and kidneys.

Neglect of posture affects our well-being. This means that we consciously make the choice to give care to the posture whether sitting at the desk, driving a car, or eating a meal. The sense of being upright contributes to alertness in the face of the immediate experience. We give equal care to the four primary postures of a human being, namely sitting, walking, standing and reclining.

## Mindfulness at Home

Look around your home and find what you feel is the best spot for regular formal meditation.

- *Place the items that you feel would be supportive for that place.*
- *A mat, sacred object, a flower, a candle, a small bell or just a chair, or meditation cushion.*
- *To begin the meditation, play some meditative music.*
- *Read aloud from a book that you appreciate.*

- *Play an extract from a taped talk on meditation or spiritual teachings.*
- *Bring your mindfulness to the breathing.*
- *Practise initially for 15 minutes and extend your daily meditation times to 30 minutes or more.*

You can practise once a day, twice a day, morning and evening. If you experience tension and pressure in formal meditation, take a break, dance mindfully, take long walks mindfully and slowly ease your way back into formal meditation until there is harmony of body, mind and mindfulness. Always apply gentle effort rather than trying to use will power to control the breath.

## Mindfulness of Breathing

- *I am breathing in*
- *I am breathing out*
- *I am breathing in a long breath*
- *I am breathing out a long breath*
- *I am aware of the breath as it comes into my body*
- *I am aware of the breath as it leaves my body*
- *I am aware of the in breath as it enters my nose*
- *I am aware of the breath in my lungs*
- *I am aware of the out breath as it departs from my lungs*
- *I am aware of the out breath as it departs from my nose*
- *I am aware of the moment(s) before the next in breath comes in*
- *I am aware of the coming of the breath*
- *I am aware of the going of the breath*
- *I experience the breathing in and breathing out*
- *Allowing myself to stay steady with each breath.*

## Words of the Buddha

*"Herein you should train yourself thus: 'In the seen will be merely what is seen; in the heard will be merely what is heard; in the sensed will be merely what is sensed; in the knowing merely what is knowing. Then there will be no here nor there nor in between. This is the end of suffering.'"* UD 1.10

*"In what way is there the preservation of truth? How does one preserve truth? If a person has a belief, he preserves truth when he says: 'My belief is thus.' He does not yet come to the definite conclusion: 'Only this is true, anything else is wrong.' In this way there is the preservation of truth."* M95.

## A Daily Reflection

I vow to remember that today is a new day
Full of new beginnings and fresh moments.
Today, I will not cling to events of yesterday nor yesteryear
But stay connected with what today brings.
I will not madly pursue my desires at the expense of others
Nor flee from challenging tasks.
I will remain true to the unfolding process of today
Without losing myself in thoughts of what was or what might be.
I will treat today with awareness and sensitivity
Even in the most ordinary of tasks.
I will apply myself wholeheartedly to the fullness of today
For I know that today holds the resource for authenticity.

The Practices

1. Five silent meals or snacks in the week.
2. What are practical ways to reduce stress?
3. Five 15 minutes sessions of mindfulness of breathing in a week
4. Daily units of 20 minutes of exercise (increase level of heartbeat) in a week.
5. Keep notes reflection on the practice. Write as much as is appropriate for you

**Write in box times of formal practice.**

**Write type of practice and brief reflection on it.**

| Monday | |
|---|---|
| Tuesday | |
| Wednesday | |
| Thursday | |
| Friday | |
| Saturday | |
| Sunday | |

# Mindfulness of the Body - Part Three

When we sustain the mindfulness, we can say we are contemplating the process. The Buddha referred to this as *anupassana* – *anu* means "going along with" and *passana* means seeing. Putting it simply, the practice is "tracking the experience." The Buddha referred to body *anupassana*, feeling *anupassana*, state of mind *anupassana* and Dharma *anupassana*.

We engage in going along with the process in five ways:

- *Keep interest, even if the experience itself drops away, to develop understanding*
- *Develop the capacity bear the content of the state of mind.*
- *Be mindful of the way things change over a period of time – short or long*
- *Acknowledge the times when you feel stuck*
- *Learn to stay with an experience for the insight to emerge.*

If we settle for trying to be in the moment all the time, we would sacrifice the opportunity for contemplating the process. We also need an overview – a vital and indispensable aspect for insight. We take an overview of our situation such as at work, relationships, making a journey, Dharma practice or life itself. Being exclusively in the moment could become a form of imprisonment.

Every moment remains linked to the moment that went before and the subsequent moment. No link has its own existence. Through the chain of links, we form the sense and meaning that would be obscured if we grabbed the moment, isolated from all else.

## Meditation on the Body

- *Apply direct mindfulness to the body to see through projections, if not obsession, around bodily appearance - size, age, weight, colour, gender and social values that interprets the body in a conditioned way.*

- *Direct mindfulness to the whole of body from top of the head to end of the toes.*

- *Moment to moment slowly scan the attention from the head through to the toes and from the toes to the top of the head. Experience directly the sensations and vibrations of the body. Take five to 20 minutes or more to go through one full length of the body with moment to moment mindfulness.*

- *Notice areas in the body where there is tension, pressure, aches and pains. In a relaxed way, direct mindfulness into these areas.*

- *Be aware of the centre of the discomfort and the outer edges. Observe changes and impermanence of these sensations.*

- *Apply mindfulness longer to areas where there appears to be a lack of sensation.*

- *Return attention to full awareness of the whole body.*

- *Experience the body as organic life, as various vibrations and sensations touching on consciousness.*

- *Be mindful of descriptions and any views about the body through likes and dislikes, health and sickness, so that you can respond with wisdom to bodily life.*

- *Experience mindfulness of body as the inter-dependence of the five elements - earth, air, fire, water, space - i.e. firmness, lightness, warmth, fluidity or spaciousness. Realise the body belongs to the nature of things rather than being "I" or "mine".*

## Taking Refuge in the Three Jewels

The Three Jewels namely Buddha, Dharma and Sangha, are important foundations of the Buddha's teachings.

Do not imagine that to take refuge means conversion to Buddhism and its various beliefs. Taking refuge reflects a natural appreciation and commitment around awakening, the Dharma of teachings/practices and the men and women of noble practice. The refuge is worthy of mindfulness, reflection and support.

- *I take refuge in the Buddha*
- *I take refuge in the Dharma*
- *I take refuge in the Sangha*

The word Buddha means the fully Awakened One.

Awakening expresses full realisation of the ultimate and conventional Truth. There is knowing liberation, an uncovering of insights into the way events unfold and an active love and compassion for all forms of life.

The Dharma is the teaching of the Awakened Ones. Dharma refers to teachings and practices that embrace ethics, awareness, love, meditation, inquiry and our engagement with the world.

The Sangha includes the awakened ones, the noble ones, the ordained, those dedicated to supporting and sharing their realisations and all those deeply committed to the Dharma.

## Benefits of Mindfulness Practice

Set aside a few minutes every day to breathe with mindfulness. This will contribute to our emotional, mental, and spiritual well-being. Specifically, mindfulness of breathing helps us achieve:

- *Ability to stay steady in stressful or threatening situations*
- *access to deep joy and inner contentment*
- *calmness of mind*
- *capacity to clear the mind of excessive thinking*
- *concentration*
- *deep sense of intimacy and connection with organic life*
- *experience of inner freedom through unfolding events*
- *harmony of body and mind*
- *reduction of stress*
- *the feeling of being centred.*

Let us look at a few examples. We mindfully breathe in and out while waiting results from a medical examination so as not to inflame anxiety. We mindfully breathe in and out when pushing ourselves hard at work. We mindfully breathe in and out when confronted with a tense situation, inner or outer.

As we mindfully breathe in and out, even for a few minutes, we have the chance to relax and to cut through much that is false within - projections, daydreams, fantasies, resistance and mind games. As we gain the ability to see through our illusions, we discover for ourselves what is valid, true, and relevant. The deep task of mindfulness practice is to dissolve delusions and reveal what is real and trustworthy.

## The Postures

SITTING MEDITATION: Cross-legged, use of meditation stool or chair without back support (unless necessary). Sit with a straight back and neck with chin slightly tucked in and hips rolled gently forward to lengthen the back. Eyes closed with the feeling of expansion in chest and diaphragm area. Avoid the use of will power to hold posture. Let the whole body settle into the posture with alert presence.

WALKING MEDITATION: Meditative walking consists of slow, short steps. The heel of one foot hardly goes in front of the toes of the other. Be mindful of each foot touching the ground. Eyes used for seeing ahead and for balance. One hand rests on the other at the abdomen. Use five to fifteen metres to walk up and down with moment to moment concentrated mindfulness. Be respectful to each step on the Earth.

STANDING MEDITATION: Stand with two feet a few centimetres apart. Hands are together on the abdomen. Eyes are closed or open. Experience the presence of whole body from the soles of feet to the top of the head. Experience stillness of posture, the vibration of life and the sense of being.

RECLINING MEDITATION: Lie flat on your back with heels together or bend your knees so the heels draw close to your buttocks. Head on small, firm pillow or two or three books. Arms resting at the side of the body or hands on the abdomen. Be present to intimacy with immediate nature.

EATING MEDITATION: Are you a vegetarian or a vegan? An initial reflection on worldwide inter-dependency that makes a meal possible. Maintain silence throughout the meal with an alert posture. Be conscious and unhurried while eating with mindfulness of tasting, chewing and swallowing of food. Concluding with a reflection as a thanksgiving.

**Mindfulness of Walking**

We bring full attention to the way we use our feet. We often think that our home is where we live, or where our heart is. Our home is where we place our feet. Where are your feet right now? Do you have both feet firmly on the ground? Is one foot on the floor and the other foot hanging in the air due to one leg over the other? Right now feel the contact of both feet on the floor. Does that feel grounded?

Mindful practice gives emphasis to mindful and meditative walking rather than attending religious services. We walk slowly, mindfully up and down, with the heels of one foot barely going in front of the toes of the other foot. This is a prayer to life, an ongoing expression of devotion to each moment. We do not need to walk a great distance for that; a matter of the length of our room at home is long enough.

If we rush to get from A to B, what is the state of mind? If we wander around, up and down, rather aimlessly, what is going on within? If we walk in a fast, intense way, what does it tell us? There is a link between feet and mind providing the opportunity for insight. Our capacity to be aware of this link matters to the degree that we can stop in mid-movement bringing recollection to our whole manner of walking. We may then continue our journey but with a mindful and calm attitude.

If we examine walking with greater attention, it may blow apart our fixed ideas about walking. Those with some depth of experience in walking meditation may ask themselves the questions:

## WHO IS WALKING?

- *Is the walker separate from the walking?*
- *Is there one activity going on – namely just walking or are there two activities – walking and walker?*
- *If there are two, do they collide with each other or stay apart?*
- *Does the walker walk or not walk?*
- *Does the walker start before the walking or start when the foot first moves?*
- *At what point does one go from sitting or standing to walking?*
- *Can we find the beginning of walking? If we cannot find the moment that begins walking, then is it appropriate to refer to walking?*
- *I know that when I walk I see the body is moving. Am I moving?*

### Mindfulness for stretching Exercises

Exercises loosen up the body, open the cells, cultivate greater flexibility and strengthen muscles. These exercises are not strenuous but practices that we can apply at home. For the full benefit from yoga, it is necessary to find a yoga teacher.

Here are some simple exercises. Give two or three minutes to each exercise. Always with relaxed breathing.

- *Stand with feet close together. Roll the neck first in one direction and then in the other.*
- *Raise the shoulders up to the ears and relax while lowering shoulders.*
- *Squeeze shoulder blades together and relax.*
- *Raise arms above head with thumbs hooked together breathing in and out through the stomach.*

- *Allow both arms to hand down, fingers pointing to the toes, stretching the back, without forcing.*
- *Straight arms, fingers pointing to the ceiling,*
- *Stand and lead the body to the left slowly to stretch the right side and vice-versa.*
- *Lie on the back, with feet close together, lift both feet off the ground, and hold for a few seconds. Lie on the back, bend the knees, place arms around the shins and lift the knees and head*
- *Do above exercise using one leg and then the other.*
- *Lie on the stomach and lift one straight leg off the ground and then the other leg.*
- *Stand straight and put the arms straight out ahead and bend the knees.*
- *Arms straight up in the air and lower slowly until hanging down with fingers pointing to the ground. Allow the body to hang for several seconds.*

Take rest. Lie down with straight legs and take rest for at least five minutes.

The original meaning of Yoga means to yoke to or be joined to –Life, Truth, God.. The great yogis of India never endorse the use of hatha yoga isolated from a healthy lifestyle. We practise yoga to learn what it means to live as a yogi in the concrete jungle.

### The Words of the Buddha

*"Having folded his (or her) legs crosswise, set his/her body erect and established mindfulness in front of   him/her, mindful s/he breathes in, mindful s/he breathes out." MLD 118.*

*"Let not a person live in the past*
*Or on the future build his hopes*

*For the past has been left behind*
*And the future has not been reached*
*Instead, with insights let him see*
*each arisen state,*
*Let him know that and be sure of it*
*Invincibly, unshakeably." (MLD 131)*

## WHO DO YOU THINK YOU ARE?

You do not have to search to make it "mine"
or go on hunt around department stores,
hang fading clothes on the old washing line,
or wash the dishes, sink full of such chores,
or find the cat, or pour a cuppa tea,
encounter thoughts on who is truly free.

You are not what you think you can define,
your thoughts become a tap to turn to pour,
you are not thoughts, nor stuck in job confined,
so join the anthem of the dawn's chorus,
abandon your beliefs without delay,
you have nowhere to hang your hat and stay.

You are not the light, nor dust on altar
nor one who has to take up what falters,
do not define yourself in any form,
to set your limit will provoke the storm
abide beyond the grasping mind so near,
and walk the streets to show what's just so clear.

The Practices

1. Practise the reclining posture perhaps before sleep or on waking up.
2. Practise the walking meditation - at home taking short steps or outdoors, normal speed.
3. Five 15-minute periods in a week of mindfulness of body from head to toes.
4. Mindful use of your hand(s). Hands reflect our state of mind, attitude and intentions.
5. Bring mindfulness to taking a shower from cleaning of the body to use of water

**Write in the box times of formal practice.**
**Write type of practice with a brief reflection on it.**

| | |
|---|---|
| Monday | |
| Tuesday | |
| Wednesday | |
| Thursday | |
| Friday | |
| Saturday | |
| Sunday | |

# Mindfulness of the Body - Part Four

Mindfulness bears a close relationship to meditative concentration. The Buddha defined concentration as unification of heart/mind. The Pali word is *Samadhi*. *Sam* means together. *Dhi* means to place.

When we do not see and know what is happening, there is delusion in the mind. The five hindrances of greed, anger, boredom, restlessness and fear/doubt express delusion. There is still delusion when we only cognise a problem but the cognition makes no difference to the experience. There is also delusion when we justify actions of body, speech and mind that make problems for others or ourselves near or far.

Be mindful of difficulties or hindrances that hold up your practice. The next steps consist of working with such experiences.

- *Name what inhibits clarity and wisdom.*

- *Do you experience all of them, regularly or irregularly?*

- *What circumstances make you vulnerable to hindrances?*

- *What would be a useful preparation beforehand?*

- *Owing to strong hindrances, do you need the wise counsel?*

- *Whom would you turn to?*

- *Do you need to develop restraint?*

- *Do you need to use resources wisely?*

- *What do you need to let go of?*

- *Is practice in certain situations a matter of endurance?*

- *What do you need to avoid?*

- *What do you need to remove or move on from?*

- *What do you need to cultivate?*

We cultivate a wise view through remembering that actions and inactions do bear fruit, eventually. There are consequences that need acknowledgement. Once again, mindfulness serves as an important function to establish a clear view and appropriate intention. Every link in the noble eightfold path matters equally. At times, some links take precedence over the others. This noble path consists of right (meaning fulfilling) understanding, intention, action, speech, livelihood, effort, mindfulness and meditative concentration. This training manual addresses aspects of all eight links.

There is not only the link in terms of past, present and future. There are the links between ethics, mindfulness, contemplation, wisdom and knowing liberation (from problematic existence and freedom to live a fulfilled life).

In some respects, mindfulness is a kind of study. We study the body, feelings, states of mind and Dharma. We treat the human condition as our university. We avoid the tendency in some Buddhist schools of the mechanical noting of a meditation object and keep repeatedly fixing on it without any kind of "study" of the object and its links with everything else. There is no assurance that simply noting, noting, noting an object will generate wisdom.

The Buddha said that we establish mindfulness to be close to, so serve our interests, to watch over the mind. With mindfulness, we ground ourselves and place it completely in front and around ourselves. We develop mindfulness so we can face any experiences. This practice contributes in real ways to ethics, seeing intentions, dissolving distress and handling outcomes of events.

The Buddha compared the five senses and the sense of the mind like six wild animals each one pulling us in different ways. He described mindfulness as the "strong post" to tame the danger of the wild beasts.

**Four Factors Contribute to Inner Peace**

- *Space*
- *Silence*
- *Stillness*
- *Loving communication*

It would be worthwhile to go from room to room at home, or in a bed-sitter, to examine the sense of space in every part of the room. It might mean simply changing the location of what is around us to provide a sense of openness to the atmosphere, even if we are living in a small area. The Zen tradition has developed for centuries a keen aesthetic appreciation for harmony of form and space and the inner benefits that it brings to our psyche.

Mindfully go through all items that give support to your body – clothes, food, travel bags, bathroom cabinet and medicine cabinet and see what you need and what you can give away as a step towards a more simple way of life. Reduce the level of input in your home. Less music, less radio, television, and computer unless you can give full attention to what you hear or watch. Use a formal posture in front of a screen with both feet flat on the ground. If appropriate, engage in creative movement if listening to music.

When we have had a good clear-out at home, we feel a genuine sense of relief and contentment.

It is not always easy to experience a deep love and appreciation for silence. Some people cannot live with silence.

Those who have a small extra room may even create a shrine room for yoga, meditation and for periods of quiet reflection. Others may use a corner of their room to keep a chair or meditation cushion to indicate a quiet sacred space.

## Mindfulness of Driving a Car

We live in an era of rapid consumption of oil and massive pollution of environment. Mindfulness of driving a car includes more than sitting with a straight posture and concentrating on the road head from one moment to the next.

- *What is my relationship to the car? A convenience or a symbol of success or both?*
- *Can I use other forms of transport on various occasions – walking, bicycle, buses and trains?*
- *Do I use a fuel-efficient car?*
- *Do I engage in car sharing?*
- *Have I tried a period without a car?*
- *Mindful driving means focussed attention, development of patience and kindness.*

## Mindfulness Practice and formal Meditation

Mindfulness practice and formal meditation enable practitioners to:

- *reduce stress*
- *develop the ability to stay steady in the here and now*
- *learn to work with difficult states of mind*
- *practise to be clear in the face of change*
- *open the heart*
- *realise freedom in the midst of things.*

We may have a wonderful practice on one day and incredible resistance to it the next. It is a matter of quiet persistence so that we treat unwelcome states of mind as a challenge.

## Words of the Buddha

*"Those of peaceful mind, discerning*
*Mindful, given to meditation.*
*Clearly see things rightly*
*And do not long for sensual pleasures.*
*Those peaceful ones, delighting in diligence*
*Who see fear in negligence*
*Are incapable of fading away*
*And are close to Nirvana." (It 45)*

*"Four things are conducive to the growth of wisdom. What four?*
*Association with noble persons*
*Hearing the Dharma*
*Wise attention*
*Practise in accordance with the Dharma." (AN IV)*

## THE POWER OF LOVE

A love not held in time and space,
a treasure with a fleet of pace
a transcendent force not upheld
and found in the most alien place.

A breakup lends itself to grief
and terror clashes, fate is set,
the strain thus met in wild oceans,
a dolphin skips the dragging net.

A love cannot know pain itself,
nor thirst even attention more,
a love is such, can't care for self,
so wise approach is just love's core.

A love reveals the tangible,
and states the way of the beyond
as dramas fall under its sway,
a limitless, true form of bond.

---

**The Practices**

**1. Use guided meditation on breath and on body.**
**2. Practice formal meditation, indoors or outdoors. Bus, park bench or at home.**
**3. Give time to silence, stillness and spaciousness.**
**4. Make any journey a practice of mindfulness from start to finish.**
**5. Take one experience in the last week and write up to 250 words to learn from.**

**Write in the box times of formal practice.**

**Write type of practice and brief reflection on it.**

| Monday | |
|---|---|
| Tuesday | |
| Wednesday | |
| Thursday | |
| Friday | |
| Saturday | |
| Sunday | |

# Mindfulness of Feelings - Part One

The grasping of pleasant feelings pushes us towards objects of attention, inner and outer. The consequences may be painful, sooner or later.

The grasping of unpleasant feelings pulls us away from the issue or triggers a negative reaction towards the issue.

The grasping of feelings between the two contributes to feeling stuck, bored or apathetic.

Application of mindfulness to such feelings includes acknowledgement of what the feeling is dependent upon and what happens through grasping.

This contemplation on feelings includes seeing the conditions for what arises as well as seeing impermanence of feelings to allow the fading and letting go of problematic feelings to dissolve. The Buddha points to cessation of tendencies, addictions and obsessions. Painful areas of human existence depend on grasping onto feelings and views and reacting to them.

The Buddha says that everybody has one thing in common: the wish to be happy.

What makes people happy on a sustainable basis?

To find happiness, it would be worthwhile to cultivate typical responses until we experience the same natural wisdom.

*"I just take everything as it comes."*

*"I just live one day at a time."*
*"I've learned not to have too many expectations of others or myself."*
*"As long as I can spend some time out of doors, I feel connected with life and don't want too much."*
*"I regard everything that happens to me as a gift or a challenge."*

All of these responses show a genuine wisdom about living on this earth. They may seem rather bland answers if we are looking for some deep philosophical interpretation to be happy. What we forget is that those immediate responses of happy people carry a deep truth to them. They are living their life according to that basic understanding and they feel the benefit in their feelings and thoughts.

Dharma teachings emphasise the importance of mindfulness of feelings. Our relationship to our feelings influences every area of our life. If we are clearly mindful of our feelings, we can practise to express our feelings wisely, observe them, explore them without reaction to our feelings such as fear and anger. Fear and anger are the intensification of feelings through desire, impressions, tension and unhealthy views.

### The Words of the Buddha

*"Suppose a man loved a woman (or vice-versa or same sex) with his mind bound to her by intense desire and passion. He might see that woman standing with another man chatting, joking and laughing. Would not sorrow, pain and despair arise in that man? If he abandoned his desire and lust for her, would sorrow, pain and despair arise in him?" (MLD 101)*

*"Better than solve sovereignty over the Earth*
*Better than going to Heaven*
*Better than lordship over all the worlds*
*Is the fruition of a noble life." (Dh 174)*

## A DAILY MEDITATION

Let us be still for a few moments,
without moving even our little finger
so that a hush descends upon us.
there would be no place to go,
nor to come from,
for we would have arrived in this extraordinary moment;
there would be a stillness and silence,
that would fill all of our senses,
where all things would find their rest.
Everything would then be together in a deep connection,
putting an end to 'us and them', this against that;
we would not move in these brief moments,
for that would disturb this palpable presence;
there would be nothing to be said nor done,
for life would embrace us in this wondrous meeting,
and take us into its arms as a loving friend.

---

**The Practices**

1.  Be mindful of feelings arising, staying and passing.
2.  What feelings lead to problematic desire
3.  Be mindful of the feeling of contentment.
4.  Is there space around what you feel?
5.  What is precious about neither pleasant nor painful feelings?

**Write the times of formal practice.**

**Write the practice and essential reflection.**

| Monday | |
|---|---|
| Tuesday | |
| Wednesday | |
| Thursday | |
| Friday | |
| Saturday | |
| Sunday | |

# Mindfulness of Feelings - Part Two

Acknowledge feelings whether pleasant, unpleasant or in between. Remember feelings give support to activities, healthy or unhealthy, of body, speech and mind.

Focus mindfully on any primary sensation in the body due to feelings, emotions and stories and events running through the mind. Stay focussed in a relaxed way in that area of the body.

Observe different and changing sensations so that a calm and concentrated mindfulness penetrates the cells.

Keep returning to that location in the body rather than staying with the story around the feelings.

Experience what is felt and be aware of any description or label of it.

Neither detach yourselves from feelings nor indulge in them.

Be mindful of interpreting past, present and future in the face of pleasant, painful or in between feelings.

**Five primary Ways to view Meditation**

There are five primary ways of regarding meditation. Each one is valid.

1.   *Meditation is mindfulness with a formal posture. Meditation is a practice for calm and insight.*

2.   *Some traditions regard meditation as a prescription, a solution. This kind of meditation adheres strictly to method and technique to enhance concentration and discipline. The meditator applies the method or technique once or twice a day from 15 minutes up to an hour to develop calm and clarity.*

3.   *Meditation is a depth of concentration that uncovers a range of experiences welcome and unwelcome. Meditation includes use of form and techniques and absence of form and techniques.*

4.   *A state of meditation arises spontaneously. You suddenly find yourself experiencing quietude of feelings, stillness, and a sense of harmony with the world around. Thoughts fade away, the brain cells become quiet and there is a genuine sense of inner well being. In this meditative space, the elements of stillness and silence become predominant. There is a palpable sense of the extraordinary presence without division or fragmentation.*

5.   *Meditation is a rare mystical state that transcends the conventional world. Some associate meditation as synonymous with an ultimate state for consciousness. The implication is that few reach this state of meditation. To be in a state of meditation is to be with God.*

Many practitioners of meditation say they struggle at times to bring their attention to the breathing or to the here and now. It seems that throughout the entire duration of time of practise the mind acts like a wild monkey jumping backwards and forwards from one thing to another with little opportunity to anchor itself on the present moment or a specific feature of it.

Refusing to stay settled in the moment, the mind leaps about from one thing to another. Meditation shakes us up a great deal when we see how little real control we have over the mind, no matter how much our ego tells us that we have a well-ordered life.

We may not have realised the real condition of our inner life until we start meditating. It is important to explore three avenues of meditation.

1.  *To participate in a retreat, workshop or meditation class under the guidance and instructions of a dedicated meditation teacher. Many questions can arise. As with any spiritual discipline, we may have important questions that we may not find the answers in books or in this manual.*
2.  *To practise formal meditation. The amount of time that we sit and meditate is as important as the     regular application of mindfulness.*
3.  *To stop for a minute or two, abide in stillness and alert presence, in all manner of places and situations.*

Meditation gives support to the inner witness so that we examine impartially different sides of a situation to find out whether there is an alternative way of looking. From the standpoint of meditation and mindfulness, the position of 'for and against' says little about the issue and more about the state of mind.
We attend to the various circumstances in our life arising from within or without. We are knocking on the door of great inner freedom of being, no matter where we are, through such a meditative awareness.

## Reflection on Happiness

A mindful life contributes to a happy and contented life. Remember to appreciate moments of the arising of natural happiness. There is the happiness of the new day, the happiness of seeing a flower emerge, a beautiful meeting, appreciation for life, gratitude at the kindness of another. Make time to reflect regularly on your experience of happiness, brief or long, and the ways you contribute to the happiness of others. Happiness is the confirmation of inner wealth, a receptive heart and an interest in the diversity of life.

## Words of the Buddha

*"Meditation is established to the extent necessary for bare knowing and steady mindfulness, not clinging to anything." (MLD 10)*

*"You yourself must strive. The Buddhas only point the way. All conditioned things are impermanent. When one sees this with wisdom, one turns away from suffering." (Dh. 273, 277)*

## ARE YOU FREE?

Are you still bound? A psyche binds the self.
Are you still tied to your desire and stealth?
Do you move freely? Or trapped in measure?
Are you enslaved? Consumed in fear and wealth?
Do you spend days in thoughts about your health?

The gods leave us no trace of boundary,
actions and fruits fly home on wings of time,
we share the tastes, we look beneath thought near,
and take up a blessed state of poet kings,
we touch upon that which a small thing sings.

Embark on journeys deep into heaven,
where love displays the realm of divine.
Yes, love the journey, *namaste* to earth,
the time has come, a sign of your new birth,
then live and love and make clear your true worth.

---

**The Practices**

1. Reflect on the significance of the feeling between pleasant and painful
2. Select a plant, painting or religious image and give attention for 15 minutes
3. Sit in stillness, in different locations for 15 minutes and feel straight spine.
4. What is your most important task today? Make this clear to yourself today?
5. Be mindful of clear and specific acts of generosity on a daily basis.

**Write in box times of formal practice.**

**Write the practice and essential reflection.**

| | |
|---|---|
| Monday | |
| Tuesday | |
| Wednesday | |
| Thursday | |
| Friday | |
| Saturday | |
| Sunday | |

# Mindfulness of Feelings - Part Three

Some spiritual teachers claim meditation is only about stopping and being in the moment. This is a simplistic and unexamined viewpoint. We can meditate on our relationship to the past and future for clarity and insight – both personal and global. We can meditate on the arts, literature, imagination as well as our feelings, thoughts and views on numerous matters. We can meditate on the realms - heaven, hell, animal, the gods and human realm. We can meditate on ultimate matters, too.

These explorations may require a letting go of the present moment rather than the constant effort to stay in the moment as some kind of absolute imperative.

Yet, we need to stay grounded. A steady and wise relationship to breath, body and feelings matters. Rather than giving special, if not sacred, significance to the here and now, we develop mindfulness of what is unfolding. The Buddha makes reference to a particular sequence, which impacts on the inner life. The sequence includes our relationship to our feelings.

The Buddha spoke of the process of links of dependent arising. These links, ignorance, formations, consciousness, name/form, contact, feelings, desires, clinging, becoming, birth, ageing and death, are equally important, all are mutually dependent. Here is one section. He said:

*Dependent on feelings arises desire*
*Dependent on desires (problematic forms of wanting) arises clinging*
*Dependent on clinging arises becoming*

*Dependent on becoming arises birth (of the ego)*

It is worthwhile memorising these four links so that you learn to catch the way feelings can trigger desire, desire triggers clinging and clinging triggers becoming (of a state of mind) and becoming triggers the ego ("I", "me" and "mine"). With clarity, we can respond to feelings, act with wise intention, and accommodate the outcome. Without clarity, the self finds itself in a painful sequence. Notice the feeling arising that feeds into the sequence. Rather than regard the feelings and views as a statement of reality about oneself or others see the sequence just as a sequence, a process that is unfolding = neither giving it enormous reality nor making it unreal. What are the dangers in clinging? What are the benefits of a non-clinging relationship to events?

**The Tendency to Compare**

Living in a competitive society, we find ourselves caught up comparing ourselves to others. We grasp onto a picture we have about ourselves and then we grasp hold of a picture we have of somebody else or others. The tendency and the picture determine the way we compare – better off than, worse off than or equal too. If we grasp onto feeling good about ourselves, we can see ourselves as above others. If we grasp onto feeling bad about ourselves, we imagine others are better off than we are. If we grasp onto the neutral, we imagine we are equal to others.

We compare ourselves with others through feelings of

- *superiority*
- *inferiority*
- *equality*

Views of differences and views of sameness arise according to what we believe - due to what others say or what we imagine. Everybody is unique is one view. Everybody is the same is another widely held view. Such views block us from seeing another, or a group of people, or ourselves with clarity. Mindfulness practice includes informing our views with love and kindness rather than upholding a Darwinian view of competition and conflict. If you know you tend to get caught up in such comparisons, then reflect on another way, a fresh way, of looking.

## Words of the Buddha

*"Wisdom springs from meditation. Without meditation wisdom wanes. Having known these two paths of progress and decline, let a person so conduct himself that his wisdom may increase." (Dh 282)*

*"The wise see action as it really is. They understand how it dependently arises and are skilled in attending to action and results." (MLD 98)*

## DON'T HOLD BACK

Do stand up, take a risk
no cost to those around,
a hero walks inside,
release is then unbound.

A diver can't hold back,
a plunge, the water's cold,
a yogi sinks so deep,
a realm beyond behold.

A singer can't resist,
as lyrics light the flame.
What does such risk feel like?

What does your voice proclaim?

As past is but a dream,
future is hanging low,
a leap remains a scare,
and trust is what you know.

So thoughts conceal the dare,
upon the edge of time,
so skip pretence on show,
and dance on rocks sublime.

---

**The Practices**

1.   With whom do you compare?
2.   Develop the practice of appreciation for others.
3.   Take a passage from a book and read out loud.
4.   Pick out an above mediation and develop it further.
5.   Write a 200 words of reflection on giving and
     receiving

**Write the times of formal practice.**

**Write the practice and essential reflection.**

| Monday | |
|---|---|
| Tuesday | |
| Wednesday | |
| Thursday | |
| Friday | |
| Saturday | |
| Sunday | |

# Mindfulness of Feelings - Part Four

Self Blame / Self Doubt

The self often pushes itself to succeed because it does not **feel** to be a success. It is vital that we acknowledge these feelings of lack of self worth showing itself in a variety of ways. These include:

- *I'm not good enough*
- *I'm stupid*
- *I'm not good at anything*
- *I can't be loved*
- *S/he's better, more beautiful than I*
- *I'm not worth being noticed*

**The Solving of the Problem**

What are we going to do about all of this? Obviously, we would be foolish to claim resolution of these major issues in a week, though it is possible. We have remarkable potential for real inner change. We can make four practical steps.

- *Acknowledge how hard it is to change these negative patterns yet not submit to them.*
- *Become acutely mindful of the tendency to self-blame and finding fault with others.*
- *Find ways to express appreciation for others and ourselves as an antidote to fault finding.*
- *Know such patterns emerge from the past as a shadow on the present.*

- *Remember that one particular feature of ourselves or others is not the whole*
- *Treat the tendency as empty, false and deceptive.*

In examining the issue of right relationships, three considerations matter.

1. *If we try to control another's life, we place great pressure on him or her. The result means the other person will either submit out of fear or get angry or withdraw.*
2. *Inquire into your need for approval. This often causes much unrest in a relationship. Do you cling to your expectations for attention and recognition that you feel you deserve?*
3. *There is a strong need to feel understood.*

If two people are willing to listen to each other and attend to each other as fully as possible then you can resolve all types of problems and difficulties. Happiness springs from knowing that we live in right relationship with others and with the timeless element. This knowing provides a naturally balanced perspective about events in our life.

There are three important considerations to bring to speech so that we approach our communications as consciously as possible. They are:

- *Intentions*
- *Attitudes*
- *Tone of voice*

Communication flows two ways. Mindfulness practice includes the capacity to listen to another and inwardly, as well. We take deep interest in our intentions and motivations for speaking, as well as take notice of the intentions of another or others. Communication requires interest in what another(s) and yourself need to understand or to change.

How many times in life have we said to ourselves "Why did I say that?" "I should have kept my big mouth shut." "It's only made the matter worse." We forget that pressure has accumulated within through the various perceptions, feelings and thoughts. As a result, the mind has been unable to hold the pressure. Until we get upset, we may not even have realised how much tension we had accumulated around the matter.

- *Are we mindful of what we say when speaking about (another) person*
- *Would we use the same words and tone to their face?*

How much time we spend engaged in superficial chatter. It is not unusual for the superficial chatter to begin most conversations. It takes a skill and a practice to see if it is possible to take a superficial matter to a somewhat deeper exploration.

What signals do we pick up from the person(s) listening to our words? Some people have a great difficulty in stopping talking once they have started. They go on and on unaware that the other person feels bored out of their mind with what they hear. Bored listeners generally put out clear signals that they are looking for a way out of the conversation.

Desire to please, fear of being misunderstood, not wanting to take blame, dread of consequences — all become motivations along with many others for wilfully distorting our speech. It is not easy to find the courage to communicate what is both true and useful even when we convince ourselves that denying truth will make our circumstances better. The more we distort our words the less we are trusted. People begin to create a certain distance from us because they cannot rely upon our honesty.

Another feature of communication concerns exaggerating situations for various reasons. We might think we are being funny. We might think that our description is the way that it was. Sometimes we simply have a tendency to exaggerate our view of a person or a place so that we say more about our state of mind. Right speech means attending to the words as an indispensable feature of right living.

## Meditation on Painful Emotions

- *Allow a painful emotion to arise without trying to control it. Regard it as an uninvited guest, not as oneself, that has arrived to stay for a while.*

- *Be aware of the difficult mixture of emotions, perceptions, memories, intentions and projections. See what posture works best – sit, stand, walk, recline, dance.*

- *Turn the attention calmly to the physical sensations in the body. Notice especially what part of the body releases the sensations, such as the abdomen, stomach or chest area.*

- *Keep softly moving the focus of attention into that area experiencing the different degrees of unpleasant or painful sensations and feelings.*

- Settle into the bare experience of the feelings and sensations coming out of the cells noticing all the changes taking place. Do not look for anything behind the emotions, as this is a resistance to the emotion.

- Stay calmly focused in the locality even when it feels calm and clear. Remember to return to pain in the cells when they sweep you into the waves of emotions.

- Any anger about a story belongs to the emotion and images we carry. Anger is reactive. We dump it on others or ourselves. Can we respond wisely and clearly to difficult situations?

- The dissolution of painful memory, images and issues springing from the cells takes the power out of the waves of emotions and the storyline that accompanies them.

- Bring calm and focused meditation to the locations in the body regularly to cool out the fire that flares up into a reactive state about something.

- Remember this is a regular practice.

- When the fires of painful emotions begin to dissipate, we naturally think differently about that which troubles the mind. The problematic emotion will have dissolved – perhaps totally. Reflect on what you have learnt from the whole experience so that drama never gets reborn in

*consciousness. Be grateful for working your way through*
*the storm.*

### Feelings and Sexual Energy

Our feelings and sexual energy bear close relationship. We live in a culture that has elevated sex into the realms of projection and imagination out of touch with the simple realities of human warmth and love. We have all become mindful of intense expectations around sex as we build up our picture inside of ourselves of the ideal woman or man.

We develop an intimate experience with another, but then we move on far too quickly instead of making time for some quiet reflection on the great value of the experience. Lovemaking can become a sacred act, a religious experience, a revelation of the wonder of life when two people have cultivated romantic love, kindness and friendship in the manual of time and melt into unitive love. Our relationship to sexuality, whether we are in a relationship or not, deserves reflection.

- *Are we content with a sexual or non-sexual way of life?*
- *Do we tend to moralise about sexual relationships?*
- *What is our attitude towards a short sexual relationship?*
- *Are we afraid of sexuality or misappropriate its application?*
- *What shows wisdom in sexuality?*

If we neglect to examine our relationship to sexuality, it may lead to pain, anguish or problematic areas in terms of expression of such energy. Relationships and sexual intimacy lack the power to inhibit freedom and awakening. It is rather the other way around. Such experiences in life can contribute to our liberation as much as solitude and vows of celibacy. In

75

a relaxed and comfortable relationship with sexual energy, we can experience much joy, peace of mind and an expansive sense of unity with life.

- *Clinging to pleasant feelings leads to desire and pursuit of self-interest.*
- *Clinging to unpleasant feelings leads to fear, aggression and such reactivity.*
- *Clinging to feelings neither pleasant nor unpleasant leads to ignorance and apathy.*

Acknowledge love, friendship, compassion, gratitude and equanimity. Be conscious of and receptive to their presence and expression.

- *Recognise spiritual feelings that nourish clarity and wisdom.*
- *Recognise spiritual feelings that fuel the ego.*
- *Recognise worldly feelings that support clarity and wisdom.*
- *Recognise worldly feelings that fuel the ego.*
- *Realise that realm of peace where perceptions and feelings have no foothold.*

(Worldly feelings refer to everyday feelings about ourselves, actions and tasks. Spiritual feelings refer to feelings connected with the path of practice or when an object of interest reveals something greater than itself such as seeing the "wonder" of a star filled night sky or liberating realisations.)

**Meditation on Loving Kindness**

The Buddhist tradition stated that we have a relationship with three kinds of people - the friendly, strangers and unfriendly. We have to dig deep into ourselves to transform our perceptions, find love, know equanimity and make them available to the divinity of love when in contact with any of the three kinds of people. It is not unusual that we experience particular difficulty with one or two people that we know. Through practice, we have the capacity to change our whole view. Why burn inside over somebody else? Why inflict suffering on others or ourselves?

## Loving Kindness Meditation

- *Be relaxed and comfortable. Close the eyes and access a warm, caring heart.*
- *Be aware of the absence of ill will, desire to hurt or hate in the heart. `*
- *Experience loving kindness towards all, including yourselves.*
- *Generate warmth to those who are near and far.*
- *Develop this meditation so that kindness of the heart becomes firm and steady.*
- *Develop the meditation despite the vicissitudes of existence.*
- *May people everywhere be free from suffering and pain.*
- *May I abide with a warm heart, clear mind and be free from pain.*
- *May my teachers, community, family, contacts be free from suffering.*
- *May my mother and father be free from suffering and pain.*
- *May my brothers, sisters and relatives be free from suffering and pain.*
- *May my children and grandchildren be free from suffering and pain.*
- *May people appreciate their inter-dependence with each other*
- *May people appreciate their intimacy with  their environment.*
- *May creatures in the ground, on the ground, in the air and water live in safety.*

- *May I find the resources for the welfare of others.*
- *May my daily activities contribute to the happiness and insights of others.*
- *May I be willing to take risks for their well being.*
- *May all beings know happiness,*
- *May all beings know love,*
- *May all beings be wisely supported,*
- *May all beings be free,*
- *May all beings experience an awakened life.*

## APART FROM WHAT WE SHOW

So strange a thing, our human expressions
that speak of matters we find in sessions,
a funny thing; we show many faces
we convey our moods and what else graces;
like clouds, we go through far more than we know,
we seem apart, distant, from what we show.
We feel our feelings, think our thought
we say what words say, yet much comes to naught,
a game of winning a point, so hard pressed,
we never know the bees hum who buzz best,
one truth or other forms such a strange bond,
we hardly know anything that's beyond.

The Practices

1. What is the difference between feelings and clarity?
2. What are the benefits of unpleasant feelings?
3. What is valuable about sharing of feelings?
4. What differs spontaneity from an impulse?
5. What feelings to cultivate and what needs to fade away?

**Write in the box times of formal practice.**

**Write about the type of practice and a brief reflection on it.**

| Monday | |
|---|---|
| Tuesday | |
| Wednesday | |
| Thursday | |
| Friday | |
| Saturday | |
| Sunday | |

# Mindfulness of States of Mind - Part One

Genuine mindfulness of a state of mind reveals much more about a state of mind than what is initially apparent. We are mindful of the feelings, thoughts, intentions, memories, views, possible projections, "I" and "my" that form a state of mind. We become mindful of the way the past contributes to the state of mind. We cannot overemphasise the importance of practice. There are superficial states of mind and states of mind revealing depths of serenity.

Wisdom does not deny the event but simply eradicates any unrest or dissatisfaction involved in the event. Your description of the state of mind matters as much as the state of mind. Your description consists of a sequence of words. There is the description and the meaning given to the description. Mindfulness becomes a tool to apply to seeing clearly the description and the described.

We apply mindfulness to all of the senses. With inner calmness, we turn our attention to objects, sights, sounds, smells, tastes and touch. We recognise both the general and the detail of what we experience through the senses. For example, we open our eyes. We are sitting in a café - that is the general. Our eyes turn to somebody at another table - that is the detail. If we grasp onto the experience, the mind begins to invest in the perception generating thoughts and stories involving attraction and aversion.

Feeling is involved in a psychological/physical process. Dependent on mind and phenomena, consciousness arises. The meeting of the three is contact. This contact conditions feeling.

What we feel, we perceive. What we perceive, we think about. What we think about we proliferate over. This involves past, present and future.

The Buddha said mindfulness is the gate to the city - namely the body with the senses as the windows of the city. Mindfulness takes notice of what enters through the windows into the city and what leaves from within the city and goes to the outer world.

The Buddha has given a list of some of the dualities of mind. It can become all too easy to cling to one side of the duality or the other. They include:

1. *Mind in pursuit of things and mind not in pursuit of things (attention, position, money)*
2. *Mind caught up in negativities, resentment and hostility and a mind that is not caught up*
3. *Mind in confusion and a mind that is not in confusion*
4. *Mind that is contracted and suppressed and a mind that is expansive and relaxed*
5. *Mind that is distracted and a mind that is undistracted*
6. *Mind in meditative concentration (samadhi) and a mind that is not*
7. *Mind that is high and a mind that is not*
8. *Mind that is free and a mind that is not free*

We develop the capacity to observe the problematic mind. We see feelings, thoughts and perception forming together. They then produce various states of mind. We observe the impact that thoughts have on the emotions. An intense mind state or experience often leaves a residue of impression. So, though the drama of it fades away we can cling to the memory. The condition of the memory may influence in unhealthy ways the future activities of our body, speech and mind. It also enables the previous situation to flare up. The more we hold onto the memory the more we live under the influence of the past. We continue to experience more unpleasant states of mind. If we go near the fire, we must take the heat.

## Mindfulness of the States of Mind

- *calm or restless*
- *focused or wandering*
- *bright or cloudy*
- *alert or dull*
- *without desire or with desire*
- *positive or negative*
- *grounded or flighty*
- *clear seeing or indulging in stories and fantasies*

## Meditation on States of Mind

- *Witness the state of mind rising, staying and passing in consciousness.*
- *Notice times of pure observation of the state of mind and times of being lost in the state of mind.*
- *Regard any state of mind as the opportunity for self-learning and insight into inner life.*
- *Witness a thought, opinion or judgement just as that.*
- *Know the difference between thoughts supported with wisdom and unwholesome thoughts.*
- *See the mind as belonging to a process not as 'me' or 'mine.'*
- *Observe the presence of motivation and use of "I" and "my" in the unfolding states of mind.*
- *Learn to explore the depths of meditation and religious experiences.*

See such experiences as the opportunity for insight and realisation. By not holding onto any experience, the heart-mind does not become the centre of existence. Realise liberation and the free mind.

## Words of the Buddha

*"If one can find a worthy friend, then walk with him (or her), content and mindful. If one does not find a worthy friend, then as a king (or queen) leaves his conquered realm, walk in the woods alone. Better to walk alone than with fools." (MLD 128)*

*"Each person is to himself most dear*
*Who loves himself can never harm another". (UD 5.1.)*

## THE VIOLIN

There's an extra string to the violin
in this concert of togetherness,
where there are no shadows
as thoughts speak to each other.

Our lives are stretched across all this,
while embryonic movements gather,
as figures on the canvas of life,
distances dissolve into togetherness,

In the quiet play of the violin,
with no alien sound to the ears,
nothing could feel so sublime,
as this magnitude of language.

In this unshaped friendship,
there's an extra string to the violin.

## Mindfulness of Generosity (Dana)

The Buddha encouraged a lifestyle of easy maintenance for the Sangha and dharmasalas (dharma centres) to keep such environments simple and sustainable. He advocated *dana* to serve as an antidote to desire. In the 45 years that the Buddha walked the length and breadth of the Sakya kingdom and neighbouring countries, his students were referred to as *savakas* – meaning 'the ones who listen' (to the Dharma). *Upasaka* is the Pali word for 'householders who follow the Dharma': - *upa* – 'up close' *as* – 'to sit'. *Upasakas* are men and women who 'sit up close and listen' to the Dharma teachings. (actually checking on the web as part of the etymology was missing, I found that *upa* means 'being close' and *saka* means 'virtue')

Through the act of listening, men and women explored the Dharma. The insights that emerged from the act of listening found expression in *dana*, including understanding the importance of acts of giving from the donor to the donee (receiver). The teachers gave the teachings as a *dana* and the listeners gave as a *dana* various forms of practical support for the teachings.

*Dana* belongs to the Buddha's practical strategy to encourage letting go, loving kindness and compassion thus ensuring giving and service a pre-eminent place in the Dharma.
The Buddha spoke of *saddaya danam deti* – 'to give with confidence'. He made it abundantly clear that the Sangha of noble men and women of practice are truly worthy of acts of support, hospitality and generosity while the giver of *dana* makes merit – meaning there are personal beneficial result through acts of giving. "A deed of merit brings one happiness" said the Buddha.
Since *dana* relates directly to ethics, practice, values and social justice (available for one and all regardless of financial

circumstances) then it will demand from one and all in the Sangha, both teachers and students, a determination to ensure this tradition sustains itself through commitment, taking risks and a love of unmeasured giving. The Buddha encouraged mindfulness of the intentions and motivations behind the act of generosity.

The Buddha said:

*"Some provide from the little they have*
*Others who are affluent don't like to give*
*An offering given from what little one has*
*Is worth a thousand times its value" (SN 1.107)*

In his typical free spirited way, the Buddha urges Upali to give *dana* to the Jains, since the Buddha regarded the act of giving as so significant, even if it meant to those following a religious view that the Buddha did not altogether feel comfortable with (M.1.371) in every aspect. When rumours went around that the Buddha expected only *dana* to go to him, he told people that they should give *dana* to those they 'have confidence in,' to those of 'upright character.' In his encouragement to examine our intentions, since motives can be healthy, unhealthy or mixed, the Buddha explained there are eight ways of giving (A.8):

1. *to insult*
2. *out of fear*
3. *someone has given me a gift, so I must give one in return*
4. *to give in order to get something back*
5. *to give because its considered good*
6. *it is not proper to refuse to give*
7. *to get a good reputation*
8. *to feel good about oneself (A IV 236)*

The Buddha said that *dana* ranked alongside truth, self-control and patience in terms of its importance for humanity. While praising those who give 'a dharma residence as giving a great deal', he said the one who teaches the Dharma is the giver of the Deathless. (SN.121)

## Meditation on Loving Kindness

The Buddhist tradition stated that we have a relationship with three kinds of people - the friendly, strangers and unfriendly. We have to dig deep into ourselves to transform our perceptions, find love, know equanimity and make them available to the divinity of love when in contact with any of the three kinds of people. It is not unusual that we experience particular difficulty with one or two people that we know. Through practice, we have the capacity to change our whole view. Why burn inside over somebody else? Why inflict suffering on others or ourselves?

## Loving Kindness Meditation

- *Be relaxed and comfortable. Close the eyes and access a warm, caring heart.*
- *Be aware of the absence of ill will, desire to hurt or hate in the heart. ` Experience loving kindness towards all, including yourselves.*
- *Generate warmth to those who are near and far.*
- *Develop this meditation so that kindness of the heart becomes firm and steady*
- *Develop the meditation despite the vicissitudes of existence.*
- *May people everywhere be free from suffering and pain.*
- *May I abide with a warm heart, clear mind and be free from pain.*
- *May my teachers, community, family, contacts be free from suffering.*

- *May my mother and father be free from suffering and pain.*
- *May my brothers, sisters and relatives be free from suffering and pain.*
- *May my children and grandchildren be free from suffering and pain.*
- *May people appreciate their inter-dependence with each other*
- *May people appreciate their intimacy with their environment.*
- *May creatures in the ground, on the ground, in the air and water live in safety.*
- *May I find the resources for the welfare of others.*
- *May my daily activities contribute to the happiness and insights of others.*
- *May I be willing to take risks for their well being.*
- *May all beings know happiness,*
- *May all beings know love,*
- *May all beings be wisely supported,*
- *May all beings be free,*
- *May all beings experience an awakened life.*

## APART FROM WHAT WE SHOW

So strange a thing, our human expressions
that speak of matters we find in sessions,
a funny thing; we show many faces
we convey our moods and what else graces;
like clouds, we go through far more than we know,
we seem apart, distant, from what we show.

We feel our feelings, think our thought
we say what words say, yet much comes to naught,
a game of winning a point, so hard pressed,
we never know the bees hum who buzz best,
one truth or other forms such a strange bond,

we hardly know anything that's beyond.

---

**The Practices**

1. Examine your relationship to knowledge.
2. What is worth knowing? What is worth letting go or reducing?
3. Keep a record for the week on what you read and the time given.
4. Meditate 15 minutes daily on calm abiding with open eyes.
5. Write out one important point from each week so far.

---

**Write in the box times of formal practice.**

**Write about the type of practice and a brief reflection on it.**

| Monday | |
|---|---|
| Tuesday | |
| Wednesday | |
| Thursday | |
| Friday | |
| Saturday | |
| Sunday | |

# Mindfulness of States of Mind -

# Part Two

A state of mind consists of feelings, thoughts, perceptions, memories, as expressions of conditions. We have the capacity to be mindful of the state of mind and its influence. Our practice includes observation of thoughts on the emotions. This week we will explore further states of mind.

Emotions confirm the intensification of feelings through movements in our inner life. An intense mind state or experience often leaves a residue of impression. Though the drama of a mental state fades away, we can carry the memory. The condition of the memory may influence, in unhealthy ways, the future activities of our body, speech and mind. It also enables the previous situation to flare up again. The more we hold onto the memory the more we live under the influence of the past.

In the midst of a painful state of mind, we tend to look for a cause. Questioning in the mind often begins with a 'why'. The way the mind responds to such a question may be helpful or problematic. Questioning can help us to understand or fuel the mind state. We need to be clear about the motives for asking why. Insight into the problem dissolves the state of mind, not fuels it. We genuinely learn something from the experience. It shows that we have understood our inner process.

Without insight, the unpleasant state of mind becomes prone to history. We will make the same mistakes again, even when we swear black and blue that we will not. With practice, we witness our states of mind as a temporary state of mind.

There is less interest in putting petrol on the fire of the mind state. There is greater interest in understanding it. We remain vigilant about its arising, staying and dissolution. We recognise that it is dependently arising and dependently passing. Letting go, clear acceptance, witnessing change and insight, transform denial and self-justification.

The readiness to attend to the arising and passing of states of mind matters a great deal. We become aware of the arising of the state of mind. We become aware of our relationship to the state of mind. We become aware of its presence and its fading away – as well as of our relationship to arising, staying and passing. We need awareness to the extent necessary to free ourselves from living out painful mind states.

We practise to stop clinging to a standpoint or being agreeable to others because it seems easier. Clear seeing or sudden insight shakes the mind state so it loses its grip over consciousness. Let us never forget that states of mind can manifest as institutions. Cultivation of desire can manifest as the corporate world. Attack and defend symptoms, control and fear, can form as a military institution. Projections and deceptions can form the world of advertising.
We have the opportunity to experience a remarkable freedom of mind. We do not have to live in the shadows of our past nor conforming to the demands of others in the present.

Here are ways to bring mindfulness to the states of mind:

- *Be mindful of the specific states of mind.*
- *Be mindful of the desire for the opposite when suffering arises in the mind.*
- *Be mindful of dependency on events, feelings, perceptions and forming states of mind.*

- *By not holding onto any experience, the heart-mind does not become the centre of existence.*

We would be hard pressed to think of a situation in our life where there was suffering without clinging. The fruit of this practice allows a natural non-clinging response to circumstances of past, present and future. If we do not hold onto things of time and change, we will free ourselves from a great number of difficulties. Through such practices, we find clarity of mind, emotional well-being and the true riches of life - unavailable in wealth, identity or conventional forms of success. Joy flows easily and effortlessly out of a wise abiding with the presence of life.

Our thoughts play an important part in our inner life. The proliferation of thought obscures what actually happens. Once again, the Buddha has emphasised tracking the inner process rather than trying to rely upon being in the moment. In his celebrated Honey Ball (MN18) discourse on psychological analysis, he encouraged clear mindfulness of the process and the arising of thought.

The Buddha said:

- *Dependent on the eye and forms, eye-consciousness arises.*
- *Contact is the meeting of eye, form and eye-consciousness.*
- *With contact as the condition, there is feeling.*
- *What one feels, that one perceives.*
- *What one perceives, that one thinks about.*
- *What one thinks about, that one mentally can proliferate (papanca).*
- *With what one has mentally proliferated as the source, perceptions and notions tinged by mental proliferation (i.e. projections) beset one with respect to past, future, and present forms.*

Essentially, there are two kinds of thought. One kind of thought is healthy, supportive and worthy of attention and acting wisely upon. The second kind of thought is unhealthy, unsupportive and unworthy of acting upon. Thoughts have the capacity to reflect in summary an event. Such thoughts can function as a useful view particularly when grounded in mindfulness of a situation. It is unwise to dismiss all thoughts or take up the view that thoughts are the problem. This particular thought with its wide generalisation is a problematic thought.

Yet, we can invest immense authority in thought, reason and analysis. We can spend far too much time in thought constructions becoming trapped in circulating ideas. These fixed modes of thinking alienate us from a rich feeling and emotional life.

**The Words of the Buddha**

*"Udaya asked: 'How does a person bring his (unhealthy) mind flows to an end?'*
*'The sensations that you feel from the inside have no more fascination for you.*
*And the sensations that you feel from the outside no longer fascinate you.*
*Such a person is mindful and brings his mind flow to an end.'" Sn 1110, 1111*

*"What is clinging? There are four kinds of clinging:*
*Clinging to pleasure*
*Clinging to views*
*Clinging to rules, techniques and vows*
*Clinging to self." (SN 12.2)*

**WHAT AWAITS?**

A murky day, intense, a fear, a heat,
a soul astray, so blind to life, its beat,
we know we have a curse, a rant, and fought,
upon ourselves as many troubles brought.

A certain change impacts to make us feel
to change our way, our view, our way to seal,
until the calm soaks burning cells all through,
and what awaits, reveals, impels anew.

A sudden view then dawns and sets us free
all names and forms thus hide eternity
unhitched, unstuck, plus a joy filled immense,
so we don't hide, nor forget what's unfenced.

---

**The Practices**

**1. Take an area of clinging and explore a different attitude.**
**2. Keep a record of states of mind, positive and negative.**
**3. Make one day from wake up to sleep a full day of mindfulness as the primary interest.**
**4. Practise letting go of a holding onto or clinging onto.**
**5. Recognise when you are not demanding of yourself or others.**

Write in the box times of formal practice.

Write about a type of practice and a brief reflection on it.

| Monday | |
|---|---|
| Tuesday | |
| Wednesday | |
| Thursday | |
| Friday | |
| Saturday | |
| Sunday | |

# Mindfulness of States of Mind - Part Three

It is simply not possible to fill the mind up with everything that we want to know about. In the field of work, study and pleasure, it takes discipline to maintain wise attention in the pursuit of knowledge. There are basic questions to ask ourselves if we have a love of knowledge.

- *What do I need to know?*
- *Why do I need to know?*
- *Is the knowledge beneficial or a distraction?*
- *If the latter, what does it distract me from?*
- *What are the benefits in terms of the pursuit of knowledge?*
- *What are the limitations?*

Often, we take an interest in one thing, move onto something else and then take up another interest. We start reading one book, get part of the way through it, then turn our attention to another book and start on that. We imagine that reading newspapers will keep us informed of events around the world. It is easy to forget that newspapers only touch the surface of issues through the story or commentary.

Some teachers and practitioners have adopted the view that mindfulness shows a non-judgmental position. That itself is a judgmental view! There is nothing passive, non-interfering, and indifferent to what comes and goes about mindfulness. Mindfulness looks carefully at what is arising, takes notice of what is present, and sees what needs cultivation, letting go or acceptance.

Mindfulness serves as an encounter. The field of experiences provides the opportunity to examine the experiences, influential habits and intentions and the capacity to make judgements based on what we can see at the time. The hunter in the forest may show great mindfulness in movement but remains unmindful of the depth of suffering his rifle and traps cause animals and birds. Authentic mindfulness contributes to ending suffering and pain, inner and outer. We neglect mindfulness when we neglect seeing into the conditions that form suffering.

When exposed to risk and danger, we may need to adopt the way of the tortoise that withdraws into its shell and remains silent and still. We may need to act in a fearless way. We may need to express our voice.

## Knowledge and Reading

The Buddhist tradition has taken the question of knowledge very seriously. There are things worth knowing about. There are things we know that are not that important. The tradition reminds us to apply discriminating wisdom to knowledge otherwise we overload our mind with information.

We may have the habit of excessive reading rather than wise application of what we read. The desire to read as much as possible as quickly as possible can block insights found in books. That makes it difficult for a truth to reach our heart. It is only when words touch a deep place inside of us that they have the capacity to make a real difference in our life. It is important to be willing to stop reading when a sentence, phrase or theme has touched a responsive place within.

It might be worthwhile to close the book for a few minutes. Sometimes the simple act of walking up and down reflecting on what touched us gives an opportunity to digest the insights. There are many lines of sublime poetry, exquisite comments on human nature in non-fiction that have the potential to awaken our lives.

For this to happen, it requires an unhurried reading, mindful and meditative so that we absorb the deep truths that are available in the text. In the Buddhist tradition, it was not unusual for monks and nuns to spend years, contemplating a handful of verses, until they knew what they truly needed to know. That knowledge stayed with them until their dying breath. It enlightened their lives.

**Meditation on Choiceless Awareness**

- *Abide with choiceless awareness through experiencing a full sense of the presence of the*
- *Allow your whole being to rest in this choiceless awareness.*
- *Experience the senses without desire to fix or substantiate anything.*
- *Know the contact with the immediate world through sight, sound, smell, taste and touch.*
- *Neither indulging in memories, nor pursuing future dreams, nor looking for something to*
- *Not focussing on the personal or impersonal, unity or diversity, sameness or evolution.*
- *Permit a palpable silence and stillness to pervade your being. It has the capacity to transform.*
- *Regard any liberating insights as expressions of reality, rather than fruits of 'self' effort.*

Remind yourself, there is nowhere to go to, nowhere to stay fixed on, nowhere to come from.

## Words of the Buddha

*"Trivial thoughts, subtle thoughts,*

*Mental jerkings that follow one along*
*Not understanding these mental thoughts,*
*One runs back and forth with wandering mind.*

*But having known these mental thoughts,*
*The ardent and mindful one restrains them.*
*An awakened one has entirely abandoned them,*
*These mental jerkings that follow one along." (UD 4.1.)*

*"Who is called prosperous?*
*One who cultivated the seven factors for awakening, namely:*
*Mindfulness, Inquiry, Energy, Joy, Calmness, Meditative*
*Concentration and Equanimity." (DN 2)*

## A FAINT FOOTPRINT

Footprints are walking in the air
the path and goal fades from time's view
while tracks are not here, nor are there,
as I touch upon what is true.

Beyond the fade of toe on earth,
no means to see what was before,
or glance at what appears to come
or points to show up anymore,

Nor any hint of what might be.
footprints reveal a slightest dent,
with nothing much for me to see,
I have no need to see what's meant.

My words are written on water

My ways do form and then they flow
I take notice and then alter,
  this change is not the last although...


---

**The Practices**

**1. Examine your relationship to knowledge.**
**2. What is worth knowing? What is worth letting go of?**
**3. Keep a record on what you read and the amount of time given.**
**4. Meditate 15 minutes daily on choiceless awareness.**
**5.  Write out one important point from each week .**

---

Write in the box times of formal practice.

Write about the type of practice and a brief reflection on it.

| Monday | |
|---|---|
| Tuesday | |
| Wednesday | |
| Thursday | |
| Friday | |
| Saturday | |
| Sunday | |

# Mindfulness of States of Mind - Part Four

The twin forces of attraction and aversion spellbind us. These two states of mind have an immense impact upon us. We can live our day-to-day life in their grip. Inner or outer pulls us in one direction and equally pull us in the other. The pursuit of pleasure can act like a magnetic force and reaction against what we don't like can lead to seething with negativity and rage.

We have become somewhat infatuated with our notions of choice. We might even think that we have a choice with regard to whatever we have to do. If there is adequate space within, then it genuinely seems like we have the possibility to make choices that are wise and skilful. Day in and day out, we expose ourselves to countless expressions of sense data, information and latent tendencies and interests.

This exposure acts as the raw material for us to try to sort things out so that we can choose what to do next. It seems to be a perfectly normal day-to-day activity. We may not realise though, that this tendency towards making choices may be having an unforeseen impact on our inner life. In other words, it is not always possible to recognise the outcome of our choices, since the outcome may not seem to be directly associated with the original choice. Through clinging, we believe we create our own reality. We believe we create our choices and we create the outcome of our choices. If that were true, the ego would constantly be happy.

We endeavour to see clearly that there is no self in all of this, this does not belong to the self and this is not what the self is. If we don't look upon things with clear wisdom, we will fall prey to all manner of circumstances. One characteristic feature is clinging. Reflect on the number of difficult states of mind that arise due to clinging. The Buddha's teachings point to liberation through non-clinging. This freedom allows love and wisdom to shine through a conscious life.

- *I will engage in the practice of not clinging to objects.*
- *I will engage in the practice of not clinging to people.*
- *I will engage in the practice of not clinging to states of mind.*
- *I will engage in the practice of not clinging to the condition of the body.*
- *I will engage in the practice of not clinging to views.*

Essentially, there are two kinds of thought. One kind of thought is healthy, supportive and worthy of attention and acting wisely upon. The second kind of thought is unhealthy, unsupportive and unworthy of acting upon. Thoughts have the capacity to reflect in summary an event. Such thoughts can function as a useful view particularly when grounded in mindfulness of a situation. It is unwise to dismiss all thoughts or take up the view that thoughts are the problem. This particular thought with its wide generalisation is a problematic thought.

Yet, we can invest immense authority in thought, reason and analysis. We can spend far too much time in thought constructions becoming trapped in circulating ideas. These fixed modes of thinking alienate us from a rich feeling and emotional life.

Here is a brief summary of seven areas of mindfulness. True wealth expresses as happiness and contentment and a capacity to take creative steps so that we:

- *Develop a caring and thoughtful livelihood*
- *Develop our mind to think clearly and to respond wisely to situations*
- *Explore ways to live a free and fearless daily life*
- *Inquire into the ethics of various situations*
- *Meditate on calm and insight*
- *Release loving kindness and compassion*
- *Work with personal problems*

## A FRIEND AND STRANGER TO EACH OTHER

I do not know you, nor your experiences,
you can't know my experience either.
I know not your experience of me,
you can't know my experience of you.
I know not your experience of yourself,
we must abide in such places so few

You don't know my experience of myself;
we think we know what's cherished and seen,
a windswept hill, trees bend and leaves in swirl,
a butterfly stays near to flowers red,
it is the act of grace, we can thus talk at all,
if we hold to what we say, then we fall.

You are you, I am I, the two of us.
If you were not you and I was not I
we could not be linked. No. Not at all,
if you were you and I, the same as you,
the same to be together as apart
then we would not know how to make a start .

The Practises

1. Examine your relationship to information technology.
2. What is worth knowing? What is worth cutting down on?
3. Keep a record on what you read/view and the amount of time given.
4. Experience extended quiet times.
5. Write out the value of solitude and silence.

Write in the box times of formal practice.

Write about the type of practice and a brief reflection on it.

| | |
|---|---|
| Monday | |
| Tuesday | |
| Wednesday | |
| Thursday | |
| Friday | |
| Saturday | |
| Sunday | |

# Mindfulness of the Dharma - Part One

Explore the application of mindfulness to the Dharma. In the Great Discourse on the Applications of Mindfulness, the Buddha referred to key aspects of the sections of the Dharma. They are the five hindrances, five aggregates, senses and sense objects, seven factors of awakening, four noble truths and an eightfold path. It is worthwhile committing to memory these groups and exploring them from first-hand experience.

This application includes the exploration of the essential teachings, including the Four Truths of the Noble Ones, the relationship of sense doors to the sense objects, the hindrances and factors for awakening.

In the previous weeks, we have referred to these important aspects of the Dharma. There are varieties of depths with regard to any of these sets of teachings.

As you practised week by week, you will have familiarised yourself more and more with the depth and breadth of the Buddha-Dharma. It is worthwhile remembering some of the sets referred to in this manual. There are bullet points in each chapter useful to read over on a regular basis.

You can see through your experience and knowledge what gives your practice support. Dharma does not fall into the category of a religion, nor philosophy, nor psychology but points to a liberated way of life.

## Mindfulness of the Dharma

The Buddha said we practice mindfulness to the "extent necessary" (MLD 10) to abide with clear comprehension. In the loss of mindfulness, there is forgetfulness, a loss of contact with what unfolds. We miss the links from one thing to the next. It is hardly surprising that unconscious pressure builds up causing the mind to push and pull in certain unhealthy directions.

We might find ourselves overwhelmed with painful situations. Distractions, daydreams, projections and fantasies obscure the power of mindfulness.

When we lose mindfulness, we become forgetful, lose our way, get confused and make errors of judgement. Essentially, we practise to be conscious human beings.

The Buddha said we apply mindfulness to purify, overcome sorrow, grief and despair, develop a fulfilling path and realise the deepest happiness.

The Buddha advised practitioners not to wander away from the terrain (*gocara* – cow's grazing area) of the four applications of mindfulness. He said that the hawk grabs a creature on the ground who mindlessly wanders.

## Mindfulness of the Past

We could not possibly count the number and varieties of experiences that we have had. We could say every sound, every feeling, every thought marks a new experience. In the manual of a single day, countless numbers of impressions register upon our senses. They really are too numerous to count. That is only to consider one day.

All of those accumulated impressions make up what we call the past. Out of those impressions, a very modest number of them matter far more than all the rest. It is not easy to have a healthy relationship with all that has gone by in our life. There are four forms of difficulties with the past:

- *What is the impact somebody has had upon our life in the past?*
- *What do I believe someone has failed to do for me?*
- *What have I done in the past?*
- *What have I not done in the past?*

The Buddha wisely told people to be aware of any indulgence in the past involving the self.

- *What was I in the past?*
- *How was I in the past?*
- *Where was I in the past?*
- *Who was I in the past?*

The ability to examine the past and the ability to let go of it reveal the presence of wisdom in our life.

At times, we experience the painful influence of the past upon the present. We are going about our daily life yet something keeps bothering us. It has nothing to do with today but what has happened before. It makes us feel very uncomfortable and we cannot find any real peace of mind. The Buddhist tradition describes karma as the unsatisfactory influence of the past upon the present. When karma reaches the present moment, the tradition describes this as the fruit of karma.

Two considerations matter with regard to the past. One is the actual event of the past. What are the details, circumstances and stories that you recall? Is there anything you might be unwilling to acknowledge? There is the relationship to the past. We usually believe that our memory of the past is acting like a true mirror to events. It may not always be the case.

Our various thoughts and feelings about what happened can intensify the memory and the pain. It is not easy to distinguish between what actually was and our perception of what was. Past is past. There is nothing we can do in the present about the actualities of what has happened. We may need to turn our attention to those events to help come to terms with the experiences that we went through. There is some risk in doing that. It is a calculated risk.

We may make the problems of the past seem bigger through focussing on them. It may take some time to come to some insight about the past so that we lay to rest what happened. In Dharma language, the resolution of the past so that we abide in peace with something unresolved means we have exhausted the karma around the issue. For example, an addict who has given up his or her problem and never returns to it has exhausted the karma, even though there is some natural vulnerability for the rest of his or her life.

We focus on the way we look at the past. There are a number of choices with regard to that. For example, we may decide to see the past as the past so that we can cultivate a real sense of moving on from what was. We may think of the past as a genuine opportunity to know the behaviour of the 'self'. We have to be clear so that old karma is not reborn in the present consciousness.

We might treat past circumstances in an impersonal way. This means relating to the events as a set of unwelcome circumstances. There is an acknowledgement of the various forces at work influencing all our lives. Such a perspective helps to reduce the tendency towards blame - either of others or oneself.

We can help heal the gap with loving kindness meditations. Such reflections require a regular commitment rather than trying an approach once or twice and then giving up on it. It is a wonderful thing to come out of the painful karma of the past and to feel a natural freedom and joy in the midst of things in the present.

### Words of the Buddha

*"One living mindfully considers with wisdom, investigates and undertakes an inquiry into the Dharma. At that time, the awakening factor of inquiry is aroused." SN 46.3*

*"How does one engage in clear comprehension?*
*Feelings are known as they arise, stay and come to an end.*
*Thoughts are known as they arise, stay and come to an end.*
*Perceptions are known as they arise, stay and come to an end.*
*One should live mindfully and with clear comprehension.*
*This is our instruction to you." (SN 47.35)*

## WHAT WILL HAPPEN TO THIS WORLD?

We weigh even more than the earth,
a plop, we sink, a stone in lake,
the sludge descends amidst our girth,
the gods now hide behind the stars
what fate of earth, of species seen,
and warning piles on where we've been,
the black of oil now runs our minds,
we dig the sand, a grave to clasp,
exploit and take, no breath to gasp.

It's not over now, baby blue,
the false imposes such a cost,
we fear at what will next ensue,
unknown, unsure and full of doubt,
the wings of birds have lost their flight
while whales have lost their strength and might
a weight of thought, a burden sears
with all astray and poles apart
and storms do strike and tear the heart.

And buried deep in graveyards close,
we long for wild strawberry most.


**The Practices of Recollection of the Essential Teachings**

You may find it worthwhile to remember several of the core teachings of the Buddha-Dharma. These include the:

**Three Jewels, Four Truths of the Noble Ones, Noble Eightfold Path, Four Applications of Mindfulness, Five Hindrances, Three Characteristics of Existence and Five Fold Training.**

- THREE JEWELS. Buddha, Dharma, Sangha.

- FOUR NOBLE TRUTHS. Sufferings, Causes and Conditions, Resolution, Way to Resolution.

- NOBLE EIGHTFOLD PATH. Right understanding (right view), right intention, right speech, right action, right livelihood, right effort, right mindfulness, right meditative concentration.

- FOUR APPLICATIONS OF MINDFULNESS. Body, Feelings, States of Mind, Dharma

- FIVE HINDRANCES. Greed/blind pursuit of pleasure, negativity/anger, boredom/apathy, restlessness/anxiety, doubt/fear.

- THREE CHARACTERISTICS. Impermanence, unsatisfactoriness, non-self (impersonal).

- FIVE FOLD TRAINING. Ethics, meditative concentration, wisdom, (transformative) knowledge and knowing liberation.

**The Practices of Meditation**

Reflect on the relationship to past, to the present and the future. What are we clear about and what are we concerned about? Practise a different meditation each day for 30 minutes.

Day 1. Meditation on the breath.
Day 2. Meditation on the body
Day 3. Meditation on feelings
Day 4. Meditation on states of mind
Day 5. Meditation on thoughts
Day 6. Meditation on loving kindness
Day 7. Meditation on choiceless awareness

**Write in the box times of formal practice.**

**Write type of practice and brief reflection on it.**

| Monday | |
|---|---|
| Tuesday | |
| Wednesday | |
| Thursday | |
| Friday | |
| Saturday | |
| Sunday | |

# Mindfulness of Dharma - Part Two

To develop further our understanding of the Dharma, we will apply mindfulness to four important areas – characteristics of existence, right livelihood, Sangha and environment.

**Three Characteristics**

During the manual of this mindfulness training, we have raised many questions. They are not rhetorical questions (meaning not requiring a response). At times, a single question may provoke a range of inner responses. We do not want to be afraid to ask others and ourselves about profound issues affecting us. We have the potential to develop consciousness to explore what matters rather than resist or become sucked into events. Sometimes the brief initiative, such as remembering to mindfully breath in and out for a just a few minutes interrupts a habit giving the opportunity for a fresh perspective. Reflect regularly on these three characteristics.

Dharma offers a direct and honest meeting with life. The Buddha referred regularly to the three characteristics of existence, namely

- *impermanence*
- *unsatisfactoriness*
- *non-self.*

It is important for practitioners to appreciate these are three characteristics not the realities. There are constant waves of arising, staying and passing. We cannot hold onto anything, nor control nor bend to sustain our wishes. This is an unsatisfactory condition for everyone. Change and the unsatisfactoriness that goes with it reminds us of the impersonal nature of this unfolding process. The process is not-self, not I, not mine. The Buddha regularly states:

- *"This: body, feelings, perceptions, thoughts and consciousness, is not yours."*
- *"It does not belong to you."*
- *"It is not you."*

**Right Livelihood**

Right Livelihood considers our motives. What motivates us? What are the consequences of what we do? What is the impact around us? This principle also applies to the pursuit of study as we prepare to enter the work place. In making the transition from knowledge to work, there are important areas for reflection.

Right Livelihood states that the relationship to others and our environment matter more than position and profit. The change from career with its emphasis on self-interest, income and position to Right Livelihood would signal a radical shift with far reaching consequences. With Right Livelihood, we need to sit down and seriously consider every aspect of what we do to make a living. It means giving support through non-harming activities. Work that is not in accordance with Right Livelihood includes:

- *Advertising to promote products or services that encourage addiction, stress and debts*
- *dealing in harmful or illegal drugs*
- *destruction of rain forests and vulnerable environments*
- *destruction of species on the land, in the air and in the water*
- *employment by the tobacco industry*

- *engagement in the research, production and manufacture of weapons*
- *excessive charges for services and goods*
- *exploitation of the poor, young, sick, elderly and vulnerable*
- *exploitation of workers – health, safety, hours of work and income*
- *huge salaries and bonuses at expense of low paid workers*
- *laboratory experiments on animals*
- *private and corporate avoidance of payment of taxes that could go to benefit the poor*
- *promotion of pornography*
- *pursuit of career and self gain at the expense of others*
- *the production of poisons*
- *work in abattoirs*

This means we must be willing to say 'no' to certain forms of work and say 'yes' to forms of work that give support to life. Some areas do seem to comply easily with the principles of right livelihood. There are numerous expressions of right livelihood in the public and private sector. We find right livelihood in major contribution to society in industry, technology and science. Yet, at times, questions arise that require careful consideration and sensitivity around the ethics of what we endorse. Such work, indoors or outdoors, at home, the office or factory, requires an awareness of our relationship to the work.

- *Is it fulfilling?*
- *If not, why not?*
- *What would make a difference?*
- *Do we feel our work is contributing to society?*
- *What is the relationship between oneself and one's colleagues?*

- *Can we show kindness, respect and support to others in the work place?*

The job itself may not directly help others, animals or the environment, but falls into the area of right livelihood through bringing pure motivation and love to the work place.

## Mindfulness of Contact with Like-Minded People

The Buddha has placed immense importance on sangha. 'Sangha' literally means 'gathering', referring to men and women who meet together to form a community of practice towards a liberated way of life. The work environment needs to develop a sense of sangha. Staff, including bosses, need to meet together to share time together weekly outside of the run-of-the-mill exchanges. Indoors or outdoors, office, factory, department store, building site or farm, there are opportunities to develop a sense of sangha. These include in alphabetical order:

- *Communication skills*
- *Exercise*
- *Group interaction*
- *Meditation*
- *Sharing of experiences*
- *Stress-reduction practices*
- *Yoga*

The feeling or responsibility can at times weigh upon thoughtful and caring individuals. Some keep thinking along similar lines on a daily basis. Such as:

- *What have I done?*
- *What have I not done?*
- *What am I doing?*

119

- *What am I not doing?*
- *What have I got to do?*
- *What have I not got to do?*

These are useful questions but they do not have to reach the stage where they become a burden. If they do, they will weigh heavily upon our life. Perhaps we need to drop the word responsibility and replace it with a word with a hyphen called response-ability. It means the ability to respond wisely to the situations without thinking of our decision.

**Words of the Buddha**

*"This dependent arising is deep in truth and deep in appearance. It is through not understanding, not penetrating this dependent arising that this generation of human beings have become entangled."*

"There are seven underlying tendencies:

- *desire*
- *aversion*
- *grasping views*
- *doubt*
- *conceit*
- *holding onto existence*
- *ignorance."*

"The path is developed for the full understanding and abandoning of these tendencies." (SN 45.174)

*"One cultivates an unlimited loving mind
Without obstruction, anger or opposition
To the whole world*

*Above, below and across." (Sn 151)*

## THE ATHEIST'S PRAYER

Let me keep heart's focus today.
Let me find kindness to negate.
Let me give and dissolve the stain,
Let me be still in face of pain.
Let me address the issues now.
Let me end this clinging somehow.
Let me express compassion true.
So this being connects with you.
I offer you a steadfast gift.
I seek to heal the pain of rift,
respect becomes our action's voice,
we face events and then make our choice;
we live in such a way and then rejoice.

---

**The Practices**

**1. Reflect on right (fulfilling) livelihood. Is any change in attitude needed?**
**2. Reflect on contact with others and any steps to take for wise communication.**
**3. Apply a fresh action, great or small, on a daily basis.**
**4. Name a situation where you need to respond wisely, and apply that wisdom**
**5. Examine causes and conditions that make a particular situation important.**

---

Write in the box times of formal practice.

Write type of practice and brief reflection on it.

| Monday | |
|---|---|
| Tuesday | |
| Wednesday | |
| Thursday | |
| Friday | |
| Saturday | |
| Sunday | |

# Mindfulness of Dharma - Part Three

We now come to the last week of the manual. We have brought mindfulness to bear on body, feelings, states of mind and Dharma. We have explored in various ways our relationship to the inner life and our relationship to the outer life. Intentions, actions and results matter. Inquiring into ethics, mindfulness, meditation and wisdom have featured week in and week out. Mindfulness practices that benefit others matter as much as the practices that benefit ourselves. The freedom to explore the depths and diversity of mindfulness, coupled with some of the profound insights of the Buddha, contribute to an ongoing transformation of our life. It is an unfolding, undying process.

## Meditation on Contentment with What Is

We can practise this meditation anywhere at any time. If we only give a few minutes to this meditation on a regularly basis, we can experience contentment with the way things are. It will help us to understand that simply getting our own way or succeeding in getting what we wish for never ensures contentment of mind.

- *There is nothing that I want from the world*
- *I do not have to add more goods to what surrounds me*
- *I practise to make things last*
- *I practise to appreciate what I have already*
- *I practise to let go of my impulses*
- *I practise to support a sustainable world*
- *I practise to show that I care for others*
- *I practise to show I am already full and complete*
- *When I pursue more for myself, I forget others*

123

- *When I pursue more for myself*
- *I forget my deeper understanding*
- *When I pursue more for myself*
- *I throw away the opportunity for wisdom*
- *I throw away the opportunity for compassion*
- *There is enjoyment to be found in what is available already*
- *There is joy in letting impulses go.*

## The Expanse of Practice

- *Practice is to free the body of destructive patterns, habits and acts of carelessness.*
- *Practice is to free the mind from greed, hate and fear.*
- *Practice is to cultivate inner awareness, to discover depths of meditation.*
- *Practice is to realise psychological and spiritual insights into the nature of things.*
- *Practice is the active work of the individual transforming herself or himself, alone or with others.*
- *Practice includes equally the social, religious and political features of existence.*
- *We influence the world in the manual of practice with the willingness to challenge abuse of power.*
- *Practice includes working with various challenges so that all experiences and situations belong to*
- *practice. At times, struggle is an essential factor for practice.*
- *Theory without practice is irresponsible. Practice without reason is blind.*
- *The route of practice is awareness, experience and application.*
- Practice is the starting point for insight and awakening. In practice, awakened knowledge manifests as purposeful activity for the welfare of all.

- Practice is the translation of a living perception into a resolute awareness, compassionate action and transcendent seeing and liberation.

## Mindfulness around global Issues

Keep in mind your essential truths that reveal ethics and wisdom enabling the capacity to respond to global issues without feeling overwhelmed by the scale of contributing to change.

- *Remember that all significant movements for major change started with small groups of thoughtful people meeting together to campaign. Stay committed.*
- *Remember to explore constructive engagement and understand the forces of destructive engagement. Remember that all suffer in conflict, physically, emotionally or both, soldiers or civilians, innocent or guilty, babies or the elderly.*
- *Remember to keep the spirits up so that empowerment takes priority and not despair.*
- *Remember to love others, love oneself through showing respect to oneself and delight in good humour. There is still much to celebrate about life.*
- *Remember that all media reports of conflict are a version of events. It is the skilful resolution of suffering that matters.*
- *Try not to get caught up in blame, anger, and hate towards those who take an utterly different view. There is far too much negativity in the world already. Blame is the first step to violence and war or condoning it.*
- *We must walk our talk and talk our walk as much as possible in our own lives, family friends, community and organisations.*
- *Let us develop the power to make change and the profound significance of realising that everybody on earth is inter-*

*connected. Let us see people, not the labels employed to describe them.*

- *Remember to mindfully breathe in and out under pressure. Don't give others power by being afraid of them.*
- *Keep in regular contact with like-minded people. We give strength to each other.*

## Spiritual Experiences

There are also spiritual, religious or mystical experiences, a deep touch of the profound, revelations, visions and major shifts in consciousness. These experiences transcend the ordinary, everyday conventional mind. Such changes in perception have a valuable place in our life as they have the capacity to open up our world, offer utterly fresh perspectives and bring about a new sense of things. It is unfortunate if we marginalise these inner events or avoid reference to such experiences as if unrelated to mindfulness. It is important the spiritual life permeates secular culture and mindfulness practices in secular culture give support to the mystical and transcendental.

## Reflections on Emptiness and Liberation

Dharma teachings consistently point to the understanding of Emptiness. This understanding requires the fullness of mindfulness, interest and inquiry. There are three primary ways for this exploration.

- *Emptiness of 'self' existence. Is the car the wheels? No. Is the car the body? No. Is the car the interior?*
- *What happens to the car when we take away the parts that make up the car? The car has no inherent existence.*

- *Emptiness of the ego. We find ourselves manufacturing all manner of stories, fantasies and expectations that fall flat. We realise the emptiness of such constructions.*
- *Emptiness of views. With views, we say either yes, no, both or neither to situations.*

Apart from silence, there are no alternatives to views of yes, no, both or neither. We can hold to views (beliefs and ideologies), reject views, hold to parts of some views and reject parts or some.

No view has any absolute truth to it. To understand the emptiness of self existence in the material/mental world is liberating. If it is not liberating, then we only have a conceptual knowledge of emptiness of holding onto views.

- Be very clear and very specific about necessary changes.
- Do you experience a daily sense of liberation?
- Do you have an authentic sense of the timeless?
- Do you have any transcendent or deeply spiritual experiences, especially in recent times?
- Do you have experiences of awe and wonder?
- Do you know experiences not bound up with self and other?
- Draw regularly on profound moments, experiences and insights.
- Make your interest in liberating truth your primary interest.
- Meditate, reflect and read very slowly and consciously statements on ultimate truth.
- Reflect on any 'transcendent' experiences. Squeeze the honey out
- Remember any practice is a preparation.
- Turn your attention to liberation that is not tied down to self and sense objects.

- What steps can you take to get out of certain habits, adherence to ways of doing things?
- Why are they important? What is revealed? What is uncovered? What is the realisation?
- You need only a few verses for awakening to truth, to reality that knows no boundary.

## Words of the Buddha

The Buddha proclaimed a profound statement on dependent arising. It is not really possible to refute such words but it clearly shows the emptiness of independent self existence of any "thing".

"When there is this, that comes to be;
with the arising of this, that arises.
When there is not this, that does not come to be;
with the cessation of this, that ceases."
(SN.12.61)

### UNWOVEN REALM

Unwoven realm, not far, not near,
Nor in between, not dark not clear,
Not insubstantial, solid nay,
Not words nor silence, night nor day,
Revealed not, it is not hidden
None may enter, none forbidden

The Practices

1. What is a higher truth?
2. What is necessary to go deeper into an experience?
3. What shows skillful inquiry inner or outer?
4. What expresses freedom without choice?
5. Reflect on the ocean/ wave as ultimate/relative truth.

Write in the box times of formal practice.
Write about a type of practice and a brief reflection on it.

| Monday | |
|---|---|
| Tuesday | |
| Wednesday | |
| Thursday | |
| Friday | |
| Saturday | |
| Sunday | |

# Mindfulness of the Dharma - Part Four

### Relationship to Time

We spend far too much time thinking about the future. Planning, planning, planning. Is the future used as an escape from the present? The future acts like a huge open space. Into it, we can place our fears, hopes, grand plans, daydreams and visions. Real or unreal, possible or impossible, this vast open space of the future makes it all possible.

We forget that the future reveals itself as an extension of the present. What shows the links between the present and the future? Alternatively, are we living in a fantasy - a future unrelated to the present? Time functions primarily as a social agreement based on the sun, earth and moon. There is the psychological time of our relationship to days, weeks, months, years and the numbers on our clock or wristwatch. Incremental changes reveal the progress of the years, growth and ageing.

We take time out to go into the open spaces to experience a different sense of things. We absorb the wonder of the nature through our eyes, ears and the air upon our body. It is important for us to appreciate those joyful experiences.

We need to understand time, as a human construct. We also need to appreciate the relativity of time through the seasons and years. The Buddha has made it clear that time is a relative construct suitable and useful but ultimately the nature of things is timeless. In the exploration of the unfolding process, of dependent arising, there is the potential to realise the timeless. This realisation truly wakes us up. It carries a liberating element to it.

## Concerns with the Future

The other important field of time involves the future. The past has a personal history to it that serves as a reference point. The future has no such thing unless we remain grounded with the present moment. We can project literally anything into the future. This sets up a major gap between the present and the future, between today and tomorrow, this year and next year. The self then again produces more questions about itself.

- *What will I become in the future?*
- *Where will I be in the future?*
- *What will I do in the future?*
- *How will I react to situations?*

## Ageing and Death

Time flows by. Youth, beauty and health can begin to change. Are we prepared for these ongoing changes? Is there a resistance or denial of the ageing process? What shows denial or resistance?

We find ourselves looking in the mirror in the morning and noticing all the signs of ageing including greying hair, crow's feet and dulling skin. We have probably put on weight as well.

The ageing process will continue and no diet, pill or lifestyle can hold back ageing for a single moment. The human species simply does not have such control over the forces of nature.

On the face of it, we seem to live in a very unwelcome situation throughout much of our life. We did not ask to be born, or to undergo the ageing process, yet we are all participating in it. The key to living at ease with ageing is non-clinging, non-clinging to the present, non-clinging to the past, non-clinging to concerns about the future.

- *You could imagine standing on the moon and looking down on the earth.*
- *You then zoom in on the continent where you are at present,*
- *the country that you are in,*
- *the town and the section of the town where you reside,*
- *the street and the building where you live,*
  *and finally to yourself.*

Taking the overview can help place our view on life in relationship to everything else in the vast web of existence. How easy it is to intensify our personal life through inflating the importance of our existence. To live with humility will help us to live and die calmly.

## TIMELESS TIME

We live in memories that blast,
upsurges from the times that clutch,
we find the way to breathe what's past
and so to sense timeless as such.

We cast aside these rocks and clocks,
nuance can come from our sixth sense;
a journey passes through some shocks,
so that the steps can then commence.

We move with such sentient grace,
a spirit free with exemption,
and left with nothing much to face,
nor need to seek a redemption.

Art forms of brush and paint enmeshed;
a heaven and earth weaves so near,
here alone we touch the refreshed,
a deathless realm we now revere.

## A BUTTERFLY

I walk through glow of sunny days on high,
I know that special something I rely;
I love embrace of soak of hugging sky,
I see cocoon, releasing butterfly,
which glides itself towards the wild beyond,
a coat of brightly colours it has donned,
and weaves and flows above the greenish pond,
Ah monarch! An insect in light respond,
as it shows brief thrust from its transformed store,
and sways in soft breezes to heaven's door,
then sails across a summer to explore.

### Words of the Buddha

*"One turns one's mind away from those states (of mind) and directs it towards the deathless element."*
*(MLD 64)*

*"These teachings of One Thus Gone (from the mundane) are profound, deep in meaning, transcendent and connected with Emptiness." (SN 20.7)*

The Practice

1. Reflect on the ageing body.
2. What is ageless?
3. Reflect on time
4. What is timeless?
5. Reflect on the finite.

**Write in the box times of formal practice.**

**Write about the type of practice and a brief reflection on it.**

| | |
|---|---|
| Monday | |
| Tuesday | |
| Wednesday | |
| Thursday | |
| Friday | |
| Saturday | |
| Sunday | |

May all beings live mindfully
May all beings live with love
May all beings live a free and awakened life

# Great Discourse on the Applications of Mindfulness

### Long Discourses of the Buddha number 22

Thus have I heard: once the Buddha was staying among the Kurus in the market town of Kammasadhamma. He said: "There is this one way to the purification of beings, for the overcoming of grief and distress, for the disappearance of pain, for gaining the right path and for the realisation of Nirvana - that is to say the four applications of mindfulness.

**One abides contemplating body as body.** One sits down, holding his body erect, having established mindfulness around him. Mindfully, he breathes in and out, knowing a long breath and a short breath. One trains oneself to breathe in and out and calm the whole bodily process. He contemplates the body internally and externally and the arising and passing of phenomena. Mindfulness is established to the extent necessary for knowing. One abides not clinging to anything.

In whatever way his body is disposed - sitting, walking, standing and reclining - one knows how it is disposed. One is clearly mindful of whatever one is doing - eating, drinking, passing urine and excrement, waking up, falling asleep, speaking or silent. One abides, not clinging to anything.

He reflects on all the parts of the body, internally and externally. He reflects on the body as elements - earth, air, heat and water. He reflects on the body as a corpse. 'It will become like that. It is not exempt from that fate.'

**One contemplates feelings as feelings.** One knows when one feels a pleasant feeling, a painful feeling and a feeling that is neither painful nor pleasant, a spiritual feeling and a worldly feeling. One contemplates feelings inwardly and outwardly and their passing nature. There are feelings present so mindfulness is established to the extent necessary for knowing. One abides not clinging to anything in the world.

**One contemplates states of mind as states of mind.** One knows the desirous state of mind as that and a mind not in such desire as that, an angry mind state as that and non angry state of mind as that. One knows confusion, and its absence, contraction and non-contraction, depth of meditation and absence, surpassed and not surpassed, free and not free, a developed mind and one that is not. One abides knowing arising and passing states of mind. Mindfulness of states of mind is present just to the extent necessary for knowing. One abides not clinging to anything.

**One contemplates the Dharma.** One contemplates the presence and absence of any of the five hindrances, the Four Truths of the Noble Ones, the relationship of sense doors to the sense objects, and factors for awakening. One knows how anything comes to arise and pass. One knows suffering, the conditions for it, the cessation of it and the way to the cessation. Mindfulness of the Dharma is established to the extent necessary for knowing. One abides not clinging to anything.

Whoever practises these four applications of mindfulness for seven years down to seven days, can expect one of two results. One is fully realised and liberated. Or, if any substrate is left, there is no more returning to a mundane way of life." The practitioners rejoiced and delighted at his words.

# Mindfulness Training Course (MTC)

*www.mindfulnesstrainingcourse.org*

You may wish to join our online **Mindfulness Training Course** (**MTC**) with a weekly online exchange with a personal mentor. This book serves as the foundation for the modules developed through weekly coursework. The sections on body, feelings, states of mind and Dharma found in the Manual constitute the models for the MTC.

You will find all the necessary information about the Course on www.mindfulnesstrainingcourse.org

The MTC is suitable for beginner and long-time practitioners.
**INTERNATIONAL CO-ORDINATOR**
Anne Ashton, Totnes, UK
For further information:
www.mindfulnesstrainingcourse.org
email coordinator@mindfulnesstrainingcourse.org

We post our coursework in a ring bound A4 paper document to those who register for the MTC. We endeavour to make the MTC as affordable as possible.

In the menu of our website ('About the Mentors') you will find a photograph, a short biography and a Dharma article by all of our mentors from 12 countries. Our mentors give guidance through an e-mail exchange once a week.

Founder of the Mindfulness Training Course, Christopher can be contacted at: christopher@insightmeditation.org

# From Websites of Christopher Titmuss

1. Brief summary of 25 discourses from Middle Length Discourses
www.mindfulnesstrainingcourse.org/index.php/welcome/eng/textsstudy

2. Pali Terms from Buddha's Discourses.
www.mindfulnesstrainingcourse.org/index.php/welcome/eng/bud_dic

3. 100 Useful Pali Words
www.mindfulnesstrainingcourse.org/index.php/welcome/eng/textsstudy

4. Articles on various Dharma themes.
www.Dharmafacilitators.org/index.php/welcome/eng/articles

5. Mindfulness in Facilitation and Reporting of Meetings
www.Dharmafacilitators.org/index.php/welcome/eng/articles

6. Dharma Terms/Groups in the Buddha's discourses
www.Dharmafacilitators.org/index.php/welcome/eng/word

7.Mindfulness Bibliography:
www.mindfuleducation.org/MARC_biblio_0808.pdf

## Useful Dharma Books.

- *Concept and Reality in early Buddhist Thought*, Bhikkhu Nanananda, Buddhist Publication Society' Sri Lanka
- *Full Catastrophe Living*, Jon Kabat-Zinn. Programme of Stress Reduction Clinic, USA, Delacorte Press
- *Heartwood of the Bodhi Tree*, The Buddha's teachings on Voidness (Emptiness), Buddhadasa Bhikkhu, Wisdom Publications, Boston, USA
- *In the Buddha's Words,* An Anthology of Discourses from the Pali Canon
- *Mindfulness in Plain English*, Bhante Henepola Gunaratana. Wisdom Publications. USA
- *Satipatthana: The Direct Path to Realization,* Analayo. Windhorse Publications, UK
- *The Buddha's Teachings on Prosperity*, Bhikkhu Basnagoda Rahula, Wisdom Publications. Boston
- *The Dynamic Psychology of Early Buddhism*, Rune E.A. Johansson, Scandanavian Institute of Asian Studies
- *The Island: An Anthology of the Buddha's Teachings on Nirvana*, Ajahn Pasanno and Ajahn Amaro. Abhayagiri Publications. USA
- *What the Buddha Taught*, Walpola Rahula, Gordon Fraser Publishers, London

## MTC CONSULTANTS

Asaf Federman (Israel)
Jenny Wilks (England)
Nicole Stern (Germany)
Radha Nicholson (Australia)
Tineke Osterloh (Germany)

# Books by Christopher Titmuss

Spirit for Change
Freedom of the Spirit
Fire Dance and Other Poems
The Profound and The Profane
The Green Buddha
Light on Enlightenment
The Power of Meditation
The Little Box of Inner Calm
An Awakened Life
The Buddha's Book of Daily Meditations
Buddhist Wisdom for Daily Living
Transforming Our Terror
Sons and Daughters of The Buddha
Mindfulness for Everyday Living
Poems from the Edge
Meditation Healing
The Buddha of Love

## Books to be published. 2015-2016

The Explicit Buddha
The Inquiring Buddha
The Political Buddha
The Buddha in the West

# Websites of Christopher Titmuss

- www.christophertitmuss.org – download audio talks and audio guided meditations. CDs and DVDs.

- www.insightmeditation.org - teachings, practices, schedule

- www.DharmaEnquiry.org - programme to deepen Dharma understanding

- www.mindfulnesstrainingcourse.org - online mentor programme

- www.meditationinindia.org  - information on retreats in India and our Bodh Gaya school

- www.dharmayatra.org Annual pilgrimage (yatra) in France and elsewhere

# Social Media

- Christopher's weekly Dharma blog go to: christophertitmuss.org/blog
- For free download of more than 100 Dharma talks visit www.archive.org (search for Christopher Titmuss)
- For free download of more than 100 Dharma talks on audio podcasts in iTunes, go to " Dharma Talks of Christopher Titmuss"
- See www.youtube.com for three minute to 45 minute Dharma teachings/clips from talks, interviews, guided, Bodh Gaya school, meditations/stories and reflections (search for Dharma Channel, Christopher Titmuss)
- Facebook Public Figure page. https://www.facebook.com/christopher.titmuss
- See *flikr* for around 5000 photos in various sets of Sangha worldwide

May all beings live with love
May all beings live with happiness
May all beings live with wisdom and liberation

46826307R00086

Made in the USA
San Bernardino, CA
17 March 2017